REA's *interactive Flashcards*™

ENGLISH VOCABULARY
Set #1 (Great Words)

**Staff of Research and Education Association,
Dr. M. Fogiel, Director**

Research & Education Association
61 Ethel Road West
Piscataway, New Jersey 08854

REA's INTERACTIVE FLASHCARDS™
ENGLISH VOCABULARY
Set #1 (Great Words)

Printed in the United States of America

Library of Congress Catalog Card Number 98-66638

International Standard Book Number 0-87891-234-7

Research & Education Association, Piscataway, New Jersey 08854

REA's Interactive Flashcards

What they're for

How to use them

They come in a book, not in a box of hundreds of loose cards.

They are most useful as test time approaches to help you check your test readiness.

They are a good tool for self-study and also for group study. They can even be used as a competitive game to see who scores best.

They work with any text.

The interactive feature is a unique learning tool. With it, you can write in your own answer to each question which you can then check against the correct answer provided on the flip side of each card.

You will find that the flashcards in a book have several advantages over flashcards in a box.

You don't have to cope with hundreds of loose cards. Whenever you want to study, you don't have to decide beforehand which cards you are likely to need; you don't have to pull them out of a box (and later return them in their proper place). You can just open the book and get going without ado.

A very detailed index will guide you to whatever topics you want to cover.

A number of blank card pages is included, in case you want to construct some of your own Q's and A's.

You can take along REA's flashcard book anywhere, ready for use when you are. You don't need to tote along the box or a bunch of loose cards.

REA's Flashcard books have been carefully put together with REA's customary concern for quality. We believe you will find them an excellent review and study tool.

Dr. M. Fogiel
Program Director

P.S. As you could tell, you could see all the flashcards in the book while you were in the store; they aren't sealed in shrink-wrap.

HOW TO USE THE FLASHCARDS IN THIS BOOK

This book contains over 700 vocabulary words with their definitions, parts of speech, and sample sentences. The vocabulary words were chosen from all levels of difficulty. This allows students to use this book to study for any vocabulary test, in any grade.

Each question presents a vocabulary word. The answer to the question includes the part of speech of the word being defined, the definition of the word, and a sample sentence using the vocabulary word in context.

Here is an example:

Question:

PERILOUS

Answer:

adj. dangerous; involving peril or risk

The hikers took caution while crossing the perilous peaks.

9/8/00

Questions

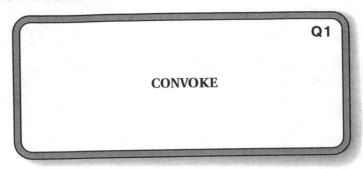

Q1

CONVOKE

Your Own Answer (✓)

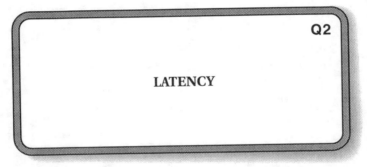

Q2

LATENCY

Your Own Answer (n)

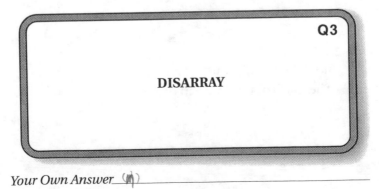

Q3

DISARRAY

Your Own Answer (m)

Correct Answers

A1

v.—to call to assemble

The teacher **convoked** her students in the auditorium to help prepare them for the play.

A2

n.—a period of inactivity

Its **latency** was small solace for the girl who feared that the cancer would reemerge fiercer than ever.

A3

n.—(state of) disorder

The thief left the house in **disarray**.

Questions

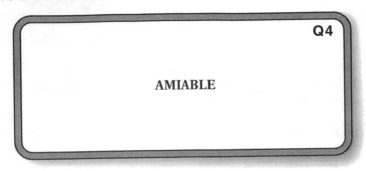

Q4

AMIABLE

*Your Own Answer*_____

_____

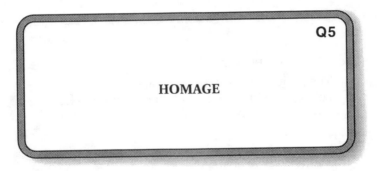

Q5

HOMAGE

*Your Own Answer*_____

_____

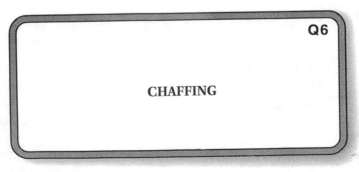

Q6

CHAFFING

*Your Own Answer*_____

_____

Correct Answers

A4

adj.—friendly

The newcomer picked the most **amiable** person to sit next to during the meeting.

A5

n.—honor; respect

The police officers paid **homage** to their fallen colleague with a ceremony that celebrated her life.

A6

n.—banter; teasing

The king was used to his jester's good-natured **chaffing**.

Questions

9/8/00

Q7

CONTENTIOUS

Your Own Answer quarrelsome.

Q8

PERFIDIOUS

Your Own Answer

Q9

VALID

Your Own Answer

Correct Answers

adj.—quarrelsome

The **contentious** student was asked to leave the classroom.

adj.—faithless; treacherous

The trust between the business associates was broken after the **perfidious** actions by one of the partners.

adj.—acceptable; legal

Illness is a **valid** reason for missing school.

Questions

9/8/00

Q10

PROVISO

*Your Own Answer*_____

Q11

AVER

*Your Own Answer*___ to affirm as true _____

Q12

ETHEREAL

*Your Own Answer*_____

Correct Answers

A10

n.—a clause stating a condition or stipulation

The governor began the conference with a **proviso** stating the disastrous results of the flood.

A11

v.—to affirm as true

The witness was able to **aver** the identity of the defendant.

A12

adj.—very light; airy; heavenly; not earthly

The **ethereal** quality of the music had a hypnotic effect.

Questions

Q13

VERACIOUS

*Your Own Answer*_____

Q14

INCIDENTAL

*Your Own Answer*_____

Q15

RAPACIOUS

*Your Own Answer*_____

Correct Answers

A13

adj.—truthful

The politician presented a **veracious** and dependable image.

A14

adj.—extraneous; unexpected

The defense lawyer argued that the where-abouts of the defendant's sneakers were only **incidental** to the commission of the crime.

A15

adj.—using force to take

Rapacious actions were needed to take the gun from the intruder.

Questions

9/10/00

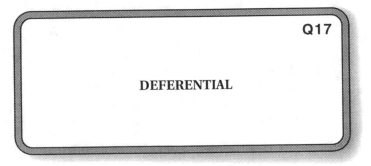

Q16

WILY

*Your Own Answer*_____

Q17

DEFERENTIAL

*Your Own Answer*_____

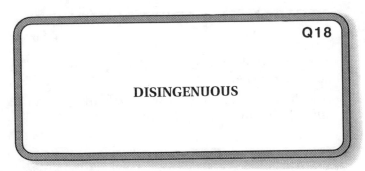

Q18

DISINGENUOUS

*Your Own Answer*_____

Correct Answers

adj.—concealing; sly

The **wily** explanation was meant to confuse the investigator.

adj.—yielding to the opinion of another

After debating with students living in the Sixth Ward for months, the mayor's **deferential** statements indicated that he had come to some understanding with them.

adj.—not frank or candid; deceivingly simple (opposite: ingenious)

The director used a **disingenuous** remark to make his point to the student.

Questions

9/10/00

Q19

ANIMOSITY

Your Own Answer (n) a feeling ↑ hatred (or) ill will

Q20

VISCID

Your Own Answer thick, slimy, sticky

Q21

ACCEDE

Your Own Answer

Correct Answers

A19

n.—a feeling of hatred or ill will
Animosity grew between the two feuding families.

A20

adj.—thick, syrupy, sticky
The **viscid** mixture seemed to be honey.

A21

v.—to comply with; to consent to
With defeat imminent, the rebel army **acceded** to hash out a peace treaty.

Questions

Q22

PAGAN

*Your Own Answer*_____

_____

Q23

ARBITRARY

*Your Own Answer*_____

_____

Q24

ECLECTIC

*Your Own Answer*_____

_____

Correct Answers

A22

adj.—polytheistic

Moses, distraught over some of his people's continuing **pagan** ways, smashed the stone tablets bearing the Ten Commandments.

A23

adj.—based on one's preference or judgment

Rick admitted his decision had been **arbitrary**, as he claimed no expertise on the matter.

A24

adj.—picking from various possibilities; made from various sources

You have **eclectic** taste.

Questions

Q25

DISPUTATIOUS

*Your Own Answer*_____

_____

Q26

DOGMA

*Your Own Answer*_____

_____

Q27

ENDORSE

*Your Own Answer*_____

_____

Correct Answers

A25

adj.—argumentative; inclined to disputes

His **disputatious** streak eventually wore down his fellow Knesset members.

A26

n.—a collection of beliefs

The **dogma** of the village was based on superstition.

A27

v.—to support; to approve of; to recommend

The entire community **endorsed** the politician who promised lower taxes and a better school system.

Questions

9/10/00

Q28

APPREHENSIVE

Your Own Answer (adj) fearful, unsure

Q29

SALIENT

Your Own Answer noticeable, prominent

Q30

COMPLAISANCE

Your Own Answer

Correct Answers

A28

adj.—fearful; aware; conscious

The nervous child was **apprehensive** about beginning a new school year.

A29

adj.—noticeable; prominent

What's **salient** about the report is its documentation of utter despair in the heartland of the richest nation on Earth.

A30

n.—the quality of being agreeable or eager to please

The **complaisance** of the new assistant made it easy for the managers to give him a lot of work without worrying that he may complain.

Questions

Q31

INCURSION

*Your Own Answer*_____

Q32

ASSIDUOUS

*Your Own Answer*_____

Q33

FEINT

*Your Own Answer*_____

Correct Answers

A31

n.—an entry into, especially when not desired

The **incursion** by enemy forces left the country shocked.

A32

adj.—carefully attentive; industrious

It is necessary to be **assiduous** if a person wishes to make the most of his time at work.

A33

n.; v.—1. a false show, a sham; a pretended blow or attack 2. to deliver a pretended blow or attack.

1. The Greek **feint** caught the Trojan army asleep and was the decisive move of the battle.
2. The fighter **feinted** a left hook just before he went for the knockout.

Questions

Q34

WAIVE

*Your Own Answer*_____

Q35

ORTHODOX

*Your Own Answer*_____

Q36

GALVANIZE

*Your Own Answer*_____

Correct Answers

v.—to give up; to put off until later

I will **waive** my rights to have a lawyer present because I don't think I need one.

adj.—traditional; accepted

The gifted child's parents concluded that **orthodox** methods of education would not do their son any good, so they decided to teach him at home.

v.—to stimulate as if by electric shock; to startle; to excite

The pep rally will **galvanize** the team.

Questions

Q37

UNCANNY

*Your Own Answer*_____

Q38

FOIST

Your Own Answer v____ ___ __ likely _____ meal

Q39

EXOTIC

*Your Own Answer*_____

Correct Answers

A37

adj.—of a strange nature; weird
That two people could be so alike was **uncanny**.

A38

v.—to falsely identify as real
The smuggler tried to **foist** the cut glass as a priceless gem.

A39

adj.—unusual; striking; foreign
Many people asked the name of her **exotic** perfume.

Questions

9/11/00

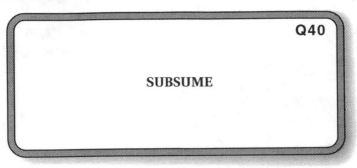

Q40

SUBSUME

*Your Own Answer*_____

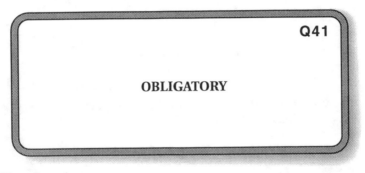

Q41

OBLIGATORY

*Your Own Answer*_____

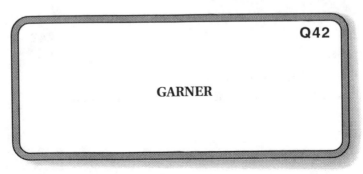

Q42

GARNER

*Your Own Answer*_____

Correct Answers

A40

v.—to include within a larger group

The AFL was **subsumed** by the NFL in the 1960s.

A41

adj.—mandatory; necessary; legally or morally binding

In order to provide a reliable source of revenue for the government, it is **obligatory** for each citizen to pay taxes.

A42

v.—to gather up and store; to collect

The squirrels **garnered** nuts for the winter.

Questions

Q43

ADJURE

Your Own Answer_____

Q44

SOLILOQUY

Your Own Answer_____

Q45

AZURE

Your Own Answer_____

Correct Answers

A43

v.—to solemnly order
The jurors were **adjured** by the judge to make a
fair decision.

A44

n.—a talk one has with oneself (esp. on stage)
Imagine T.S. Eliot's poem "The Waste Land"
performed on stage as a kind of **soliloquy**!

A45

adj.—the clear blue color of the sky
The **azure** sky made the picnic day perfect.

Questions

9/12/00

Q46

ALTRUISTIC

Your Own Answer Unselfish

Q47

PALLOR

Your Own Answer

Q48

EQUANIMITY

Your Own Answer

Correct Answers

A46

adj.—unselfish

The **altruistic** volunteer donated much time and energy in an effort to raise funds for the children's hospital.

A47

n.—lack of facial color

The more vivid the testimony grew, the more the witness seemed to take on a ghostly **pallor**.

A48

n.—the quality of remaining calm and undisturbed

Equanimity can be reached when stress is removed from life.

Questions

9/12/00

```
                                              Q49

              EMULATE
```

*Your Own Answer*_____

_____

```
                                              Q50

              UNIVERSAL
```

*Your Own Answer*_____

_____

```
                                              Q51

              RELEGATE
```

*Your Own Answer*_____

_____

Correct Answers

A49

v.—to try to equal or excel

The neophyte teacher was hoping to **emulate** her mentor.

A50

adj.—concerning everyone; existing everywhere

Pollution does not affect just one country or state—it's a **universal** problem.

A51

v.—to banish; to put to a lower position

With Internal Affairs launching an investigation into charges that Officer Wicker had harassed a suspect, he was **relegated** to desk duty.

Questions

9/13/00

Q52

GAFFE

Your Own Answer_____

Q53

OBVIATE

Your Own Answer_____

Q54

UMBRAGE

Your Own Answer_____

Correct Answers

A52

n.—a blunder

Calling the woman by the wrong name was a huge **gaffe**.

A53

v.—to make unnecessary

The invention of cars has **obviated** the use of horse and carriage.

A54

n.—offense or resentment

The candidate took **umbrage** at the remark of his opponent.

Questions

Q55

ARDENT

*Your Own Answer*_____

Q56

EPHEMERAL

*Your Own Answer*_____

Q57

DELIBERATE

*Your Own Answer*_____

Correct Answers

A55

adj.—with passionate or intense feelings

The fans' **ardent** love of the game kept them returning to watch the terrible team.

A56

adj.—very short-lived; lasting only a short time

Living alone gave him an **ephemeral** happiness, soon to be replaced with utter loneliness.

A57

v.; adj.—1. to consider carefully; to weigh in the mind 2. intentional

1. The jury **deliberated** for three days before reaching a verdict.

2. The brother's **deliberate** attempt to get his sibling blamed for his mistake was obvious to all.

Questions

10/18/00

Q58

RESOLUTION ✓

Your Own Answer (n.) proposal, promise determination

Q59

LAMBENT

Your Own Answer

Q60

COMPATIBLE

Your Own Answer

Correct Answers

A58

n.—proposal; promise; determination

Former U.S. Senator George Mitchell journeyed to Ireland to help bring about a peaceful **resolution** to years of strife.

A59

adj.—traveling gently over a surface; flickering

The **lambent** flame lit the dark room as the breeze wafted in.

A60

adj.—in agreement with; harmonious

When repairing an automobile, it is necessary to use parts **compatible** with its make and model.

Questions

EXTEMPORIZE

*Your Own Answer*_____

DIVERSE

*Your Own Answer*_____

CACHE

*Your Own Answer*_____

Correct Answers

A61

v.—to improvise; to make it up as you go along

It was necessary for the musician to **extemporize** when his music fell off the stand.

A62

adj.—different; varied

The course offerings were so **diverse** I had a tough time choosing.

A63

n.—stockpile; store; heap; hiding place for goods

The town kept a **cache** of salt on hand to melt winter's snow off the roads.

Questions

Q64

AMISS

*Your Own Answer*_____

Q65

EDIFY

*Your Own Answer*_____

Q66

PRESCRIPTIVE

*Your Own Answer*_____

Correct Answers

adj.; adv.—1. wrong; awry; wrongly 2. in a defective manner

1. He was **amiss** to see that his jacket was gone.

2. Its new muffler aside, the car was behaving **amiss**.

v.—to build or establish; to instruct and improve the mind

According to their schedule, the construction company will **edify** the foundation of the building in one week.

adj.—done by custom; unbending

At the heart of the Australian aborigines' **prescriptive** coming-of-age rite for men is a walkabout.

Questions

Q67

GLOAT

*Your Own Answer*_____

Q68

DEXTEROUS

*Your Own Answer*_____

Q69

PROSAIC

*Your Own Answer*_____

Correct Answers

A67

v.—to brag, to glory over
She **gloated** over the fact that she received the highest score on the exam, annoying her classmates to no end.

A68

adj.—skillful; quick mentally or physically
The **dexterous** gymnast was the epitome of grace on the balance beam.

A69

adj.—tiresome; ordinary
He wanted to do something new; he was tired of the **prosaic** activities his parents suggested each day.

Questions

Q70

FORBEARANCE

*Your Own Answer*_____

Q71

SERVILE

*Your Own Answer*_____

Q72

FOSTER

*Your Own Answer*_____

Correct Answers

n.—<u>patience</u>; self-restraint

He exhibited remarkable (forbearance) when confronted with the mischievous children.

slavishly obsequious

adj.—(slavish); groveling

He knew they both possessed equal abilities, and yet he was always treated as a **servile** underling.

v.—to encourage; to nurture; to support

A good practice routine (fosters) success.

Questions

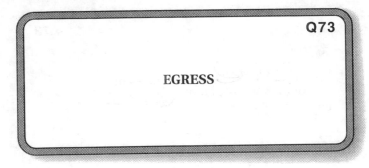

Q73

EGRESS

Your Own Answer_____

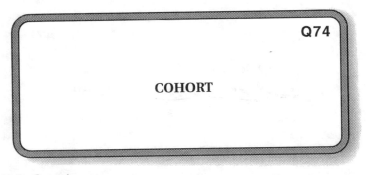

Q74

COHORT

Your Own Answer_____

Q75

OSTENSIBLE

Your Own Answer_____

Correct Answers

A73

n.—a way out; exit
The doorway provided an **egress** from the chamber.

A74

n.—a group; band
The **cohort** of teens gathered at the athletic field.

A75

adj.—apparent
The **ostensible** reason for choosing the girl was for her beauty.

Questions

Q76

SARCASM

*Your Own Answer*_____

_____

Q77

HOMEOSTASIS

*Your Own Answer*_____

_____

Q78

NOISOME

*Your Own Answer*_____

_____

Correct Answers

A76

n.—ironic, bitter humor designed to wound

The teacher did not appreciate the student's (sarcasm) and gave him detention.

A77

n.—maintenance of stability

Knowing the seriousness of the operation, the surgeons were concerned about restoring the patient to **homeostasis**.

A78

adj.—harmful to health; having a foul odor

The noisome food was the cause of their illness.

Questions

Q79

SOMBER

*Your Own Answer*_____

_____

Q80

TRIVIAL

*Your Own Answer*_____

_____

Q81

ANOINT

*Your Own Answer*_____

_____

Correct Answers

adj.—dark and depressing; gloomy
The sad story had put everyone in a **somber** mood.

adj.—unimportant; small; worthless
Although her mother felt otherwise, she considered her dishwashing chore **trivial**.

v.—to crown; to ordain
A member of the monarchy was **anointed** by the king.

Questions

Q82

SLOTH

*Your Own Answer*_____

_____

Q83

PERDITION

*Your Own Answer*_____

_____

Q84

SEDENTARY

*Your Own Answer*_____

_____

Correct Answers

A82

n.—disinclination to action or labor; a slow-moving, tree-dwelling mammal of Central and South America.

His lazy, couch potato lifestyle gave him the reputation for being a sloth.

A83

n.—ruination
The perdition of the building was caused by the strong quake.

A84

adj.—characterized by sitting; remaining in one locality
The sedentary child had not moved after two hours.

Questions

Q85

SEDULOUS

*Your Own Answer*_____

_____

Q86

GAINSAY

*Your Own Answer*_____

_____

Q87

PALLID

*Your Own Answer*_____

_____

Correct Answers

A85

adj.—working diligently; persistent
The sedulous habits of the team will surely
conclude in victory.

A86

v.—to speak against; to contradict; to deny
With Senator Bowker the only one to gainsay it,
the bill passed overwhelmingly.

A87

adj.—pale in color
The visitor left the hospital room with a pallid
face.

Questions

Q88

Q88

INCOGNITO

*Your Own Answer*_____

Q89

GARISH

*Your Own Answer*_____

Q90

CONUNDRUM

*Your Own Answer*_____

Correct Answers

A88

adj.—unidentified; disguised; concealed
The federal Witness Protection Program makes its charges permanently **incognito**.

A89

adj.—gaudy, showy
The gold fixtures seemed **garish**.

A90

n.—a puzzle or riddle
I spent two hours trying to figure out the **conundrum**.

Questions

Q91

OBLITERATE

*Your Own Answer*_____

Q92

RECALCITRANT

*Your Own Answer*_____

Q93

SALUTATORY

*Your Own Answer*_____

Correct Answers

A91

v.—to destroy completely

Poaching nearly **obliterated** the world's whale population.

A92

adj.—stubbornly rebellious

The boy became **recalcitrant** when the curfew was enforced.

A93

adj.—of or containing greetings

Two messengers were sent to the new neighbors with a **salutatory** letter.

Questions

Q94

AUDACIOUS

(adj.) fearless, bold

Your Own Answer The audacious soldier went ~~into the~~ battle without a shield.

Q95

PIED

(adj.) colored, blotched together

Your Own Answer The extream heam caused the colors ~~blotched together~~, & become

Q96

BEHOLDEN

(adj.) indebted to

Your Own Answer

Correct Answers

A94

adj.—fearless; bold

The **audacious** soldier went into battle without a shield.

A95

adj.—colored, blotched together

The extreme heat caused the colors to become **pied**.

A96

adj.—indebted to

The children were **beholden** to their parents for the car loan.

Questions

Q97

DISINTERESTED

(adj) neutral, unbiased (uninterested)

Your Own Answer A disinterested person needed
to serve as arbitrator of the argument.

Q98

FRAUGHT

(adj) loaded, charged.

Your Own Answer The comment was fraught
with sarcasm

Q99

YOKE

(n) harness, collar
(v) to bond or link together.

Your Own Answer

Correct Answers

A97

adj.—neutral; unbiased (alternate meaning: uninterested)

A **disinterested** person was needed to serve as arbitrator of the argument.

A98

adj.—loaded; charged

The comment was **fraught** with sarcasm.

A99

n.; v.—1. harness; collar 2. to bond or link together

1. The jockey led her horse by the **yoke** around its neck and face.
2. The farmer **yoked** the oxen and set out to plow his fields

Questions

Q100

PAUCITY

*Your Own Answer*_____

Q101

FULSOME

*Your Own Answer*_____

Q102

STUPOR

*Your Own Answer*_____

Correct Answers

A100

n.—scarcity

The described feast was actually a buffet with a **paucity** of food.

A101

adj.—disgusting due to excess

The man became obese when he indulged in **fulsome** eating.

A102

n.—a stunned or bewildered condition

He was in a **stupor** after being hit on the head.

Questions

Q103

DISAVOW ✓

Your Own Answer Ⓥ to deny,

Q104

ABHOR

Your Own Answer Ⓥ to hate

Q105

STRIATED

Your Own Answer (adj.) having lines

Correct Answers

A103

v.—to deny; to refuse to acknowledge

The actor has **disavowed** the rumor.

A104

v.—to hate

By the way her jaw tensed when he walked in, it is easy to see that she **abhors** him.

A105

adj.—having lines or grooves

The **striated** road was ready for traffic.

Questions

Q106

LACONIC

Your Own Answer (adj) sparing of words.

Q107

SPENDTHRIFT

Your Own Answer (n) a person spends money extravagantly

Q108

VIRILE

Your Own Answer (adj) Masculine

Correct Answers

A106

adj.—sparing of words; terse, pithy
After a **laconic** introduction the program began.

A107

n.—a person who spends money extravagantly
The **spendthrift** bought two new necklaces and three pairs of shoes.

A108

adj.—characteristic of a man; masculine
Strong muscles and wide shoulders are only a few characteristics that identify him as a **virile** young man.

Questions

Q109

RHAPSODIZE

Your Own Answer (V) to speak or write in a very enthusiastic manner

---

Q110

PROTOCOL

Your Own Answer (n) Record of Documents, (OR) original draft.

Q111

MENAGERIE

Your Own Answer (n) a place to keep (or) strange animals

Correct Answers

A109

v.—to speak or write in a very enthusiastic manner

Hearing the general **rhapsodize** about his time as a plebe sent a wave of recognition through the academy grads.

A110

n.—an original draft or record of a document

The **protocol** was given to the president once it was completed.

A111

n.—a place to keep or a collection of wild or strange animals

Little Ryan couldn't wait to visit the zoo to see the **menagerie** of wild boars.

Questions

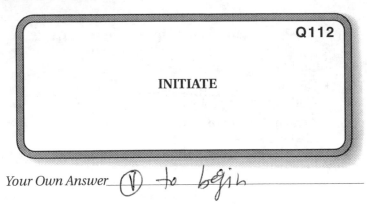

Q112

INITIATE

Your Own Answer (V) to begin

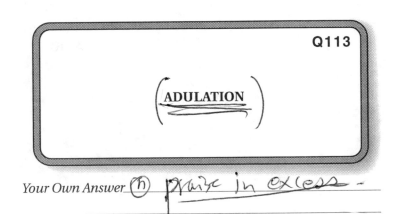

Q113

ADULATION

Your Own Answer (n) praise in excess –

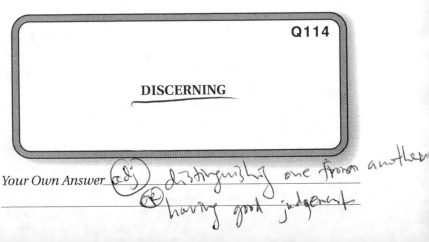

Q114

DISCERNING

Your Own Answer (adj) distinguishing one from another
OR having good judgement

Correct Answers

v.; n.—1. to begin; to admit into a group **A112**
2. a person who is in the process of being admitted into a group

1. He **initiated** the dinner discussion by asking his father to borrow the car.

2. As an **initiate** to the Explorers, George was expected to have a taste for the outdoor life.

A113

n.—praise in excess
The **adulation** was in response to the heroic feat.

A114

adj.—distinguishing one thing from another; having good judgment
He has a **discerning** eye for knowing the original from the copy.

Questions

Q115

EDIFICE

Your Own Answer (N) a large building

Q116

ALLEVIATE ↓

Your Own Answer (V) to ~~lesse~~ lessen or make easier -

Q117

INCOHERENT ✓

Your Own Answer (adj) illogical, Rambling disjointed.

Correct Answers

n.—a large building
The **edifice** rose 20 stories and spanned two blocks.

v.—to lessen or make easier
The airport's monorail **alleviates** vehicular traffic.

adj.—illogical; rambling; disjointed
Following the accident, the woman went into shock and became **incoherent** as medics struggled to understand her.

Questions

Q118

BESEECH

Your Own Answer (V) to ask earnestly ✓

Q119

LIMBER

Your Own Answer (adj) flexible

Q120

CANDID ✓

Your Own Answer (adj) truthful, honest, sincere;

Correct Answers

A118

v.—to ask earnestly
The soldiers **beseeched** the civilians for help.

A119

adj.—flexible; pliant
The dancers must be **limber** to do their ballet steps.

A120

adj.—honest; truthful; sincere
People trust her because she's so **candid**.

Questions

Q121

IMPIETY

Your Own Answer_____

Q122

CORPULENCE

Your Own Answer_____

Q123

PROVERBIAL ✓

Your Own Answer (adj.) well known because it is frequently referred to.

Correct Answers

A121

n.—irreverence toward God; lack of respect

The bishop condemned the **impiety** of the celebrity's assertions.

A122

n.—obesity

The **corpulence** of the man kept him from fitting into the seat.

A123

adj.—well-known because it is commonly referred to

King Solomon's **proverbial** wisdom has been admired through the ages.

Questions

PRESCIENCE

*Your Own Answer*_____

TACITURN

*Your Own Answer*_____

CLOTURE

*Your Own Answer*_____

Correct Answers

A124

n.—knowing about something before it happens

The morning of the big game I had a **prescience** that we would win.

A125

adj.—inclined to silence; speaking little; dour, stern

The man was so **taciturn** it was forgotten that he was there.

A126

n.—a parliamentary procedure to end debate and begin to vote

Cloture was declared as the parliamentarians readied to register their votes.

Questions

TROTH

*Your Own Answer*_____

_____

ODIUM

*Your Own Answer*_____

_____

MENDACIOUS

*Your Own Answer*_____

_____

Correct Answers

A127

n.—belief; faith; fidelity

The couple pledged **troth** to each other through their vows.

A128

n.—a hate; the disgrace from a hateful action

Odium could be felt for the man who destroyed the school.

A129

adj.—not truthful; lying

The couple was swindled out of their life's savings by the **mendacious** con men.

Questions

Q130

PERILOUS

*Your Own Answer*_____

_____

Q131

DISENTANGLE

*Your Own Answer*_____

_____

Q132

TUTELAGE

*Your Own Answer*_____

_____

Correct Answers

A130

adj.—dangerous; involving peril or risk

The hikers took caution while crossing the **perilous** peaks.

A131

v.—to free from confusion

We need to **disentangle** ourselves from the dizzying variety of choices.

A132

n.—the condition of being under a guardian or a tutor

Being under the **tutelage** of a master musician is a great honor.

Questions

Q133

PARAPHERNALIA

*Your Own Answer*_____

Q134

AUGUST

*Your Own Answer*_____

Q135

ESTIMABLE

*Your Own Answer*_____

Correct Answers

A133

n.—equipment; accessories
She looked guilty since the drug **paraphernalia**
was found in her apartment.

A134

adj.—to be imposing or magnificent
The palace was **august** in gold and crystal.

A135

adj.—deserving respect
The **estimable** hero was given a parade.

Questions

Q136

SUPPLIANT

*Your Own Answer*_____

_____

Q137

MORDANT

*Your Own Answer*_____

_____

Q138

WREAK

*Your Own Answer*_____

_____

Correct Answers

A136

adj.—asking earnestly and submissively

Her **suppliant** request of wanting to know the name of the man was met with a laugh.

A137

adj.—cutting; sarcastic

Her **mordant** remark made me feel unqualified and useless.

A138

v.—to give vent; to inflict

The dragon will **wreak** havoc upon the country-side.

Questions

PROVOCATIVE

*Your Own Answer*_____

DISPARATE

*Your Own Answer*_____

INDELIBLE

*Your Own Answer*_____

Correct Answers

A139

adj.—tempting; irritating

Pop singer Madonna has been criticized for her **provocative** clothing and music lyrics.

A140

adj.—unequal; dissimilar; different

They came from **disparate** backgrounds, one a real estate magnate, the other a custodian.

A141

adj.—that which cannot be blotted out or erased

The photograph of Neil Armstrong setting foot on the moon made an **indelible** impression on all who saw it.

Questions

Q142

OLIGARCHY

*Your Own Answer*_____

Q143

MOTIF

*Your Own Answer*_____

Q144

NEFARIOUS

*Your Own Answer*_____

Correct Answers

A142

n.—form of government in which the supreme power is placed in the hands of a small, exclusive group

The **oligarchy** took control after the king was overthrown.

A143

n.—theme

Although the college students lived in Alaska, they decided on a tropical **motif** for their dorm room.

A144

adj.—being villainous or wicked

The **nefarious** ruler hoarded all of the food and let his subjects starve.

Questions

Q145

SORDID

*Your Own Answer*_____

Q146

SHOAL

*Your Own Answer*_____

Q147

DISDAIN

*Your Own Answer*_____

Correct Answers

adj.—filthy; base; vile

The **sordid** gutters needed to be cleaned after the long, rainy autumn.

n.—a large group or crowd

Shoals of grain were stored in the barn.

n.; v.—1. intense dislike 2. to look down upon; to scorn

1. She **disdains** the very ground you walk upon.

2. She showed great **disdain** toward anyone who did not agree with her.

Questions

Q148

FUTILE

*Your Own Answer*_____

Q149

INCREDULOUS

*Your Own Answer*_____

Q150

MESMERIZE

*Your Own Answer*_____

Correct Answers

A148

adj.—worthless; unprofitable
It was a **futile** decision to invest in that company since they never made any money.

A149

adj.—skeptical
The **incredulous** look on his face led me to believe he was not convinced of its importance.

A150

v.—to hypnotize
The swaying motion of the swing **mesmerized** the baby into a deep sleep.

Questions

Q151

VITIATE

*Your Own Answer*_____

Q152

FLOUT

*Your Own Answer*_____

Q153

INTERMITTENT

*Your Own Answer*_____

Correct Answers

v.—to spoil; to cause moral weakness

A rainstorm will **vitiate** our plans for a day of hiking.

v.—to mock or jeer

Do not **flout** an opponent if you believe in fair play.

adj.—periodic; occasional

Luckily, the snow was only **intermittent**, so the accumulation was slight.

Questions

Q154

TRANQUILLITY

*Your Own Answer*_____

Q155

PROBLEMATIC

*Your Own Answer*_____

Q156

DEVOID

*Your Own Answer*_____

Correct Answers

n.—peace; stillness; harmony

The **tranquillity** of the tropical island was reflected in its calm blue waters and warm sunny climate.

adj.—being hard to deal with; unsolved situation

The constant squeak of the door was **problematic**.

adj.—lacking; empty

The interplanetary probe indicated that the planet was **devoid** of any atmosphere.

Questions

Q157

FEALTY

*Your Own Answer*_____

Q158

CONCEIT

*Your Own Answer*_____

Q159

AVIARY

*Your Own Answer*_____

Correct Answers

A157

n.—loyalty

The baron was given land in exchange for his **fealty** to the king.

A158

n.—an exaggerated personal opinion

The man's belief that he was the best player on the team was pure **conceit**.

A159

n.—a large place to keep birds

The birds were being housed in the **aviary**.

Questions

Q160

WELTER

*Your Own Answer*_____

Q161

INCISIVE

*Your Own Answer*_____

Q162

ENCUMBER

*Your Own Answer*_____

Correct Answers

v.; n.—1. to roll about or wallow; to soak or **A160**
bathe; to be tumbled or tossed at sea 2. a
confusion; turmoil

1. The pigs **welter** in the mud to cool off since they
do not have sweat glands.
2. When the emergency alarm sounded, a **welter** of
shivering office workers formed in the street as
people evacuated the site.

A161

adj.—getting to the heart of things; to the point

His **incisive** questioning helped settle the
matter quickly.

A162

v.—to hold back; to hinder; to burden, load
down

The review of the ethics committee **encum-
bered** the deal from being finalized.

Questions

Q163

COTERIE

*Your Own Answer*_____

_____

Q164

IMPERIOUS

*Your Own Answer*_____

_____

Q165

CANT

*Your Own Answer*_____

_____

Correct Answers

n.—a clique; a group who meet frequently, usually socially

A special aspect of campus life is joining a **coterie**.

adj.—arrogant; urgent

Her **imperious** manner cost her her two best friends.

n.; v.—1. insincere or hypocritical statements of high ideals; the jargon of a particular group or occupation; sloping or slanting surface 2. to give a sloping surface; to tilt; to throw off or out by tilting

1. The theater majors had difficulty understanding the **cant** of the computer scientists.
2. The roofer **canted** the board so the water would run off.

Questions

Q166

RUMMAGE

*Your Own Answer*_____

Q167

DEPLETE

*Your Own Answer*_____

Q168

EFFERVESCENCE

*Your Own Answer*_____

Correct Answers

A166

v.; n.—1. to search thoroughly 2. miscellaneous articles; odds and ends

1. Determined to find his college yearbook, he **rummaged** through every box in the garage.
2. Once all the **rummage** was cleared out, he began to redecorate the attic space.

A167

v.—to reduce; to empty, exhaust

Having to pay the entire bill will **deplete** the family's savings.

A168

n.—liveliness; spirit; enthusiasm; bubbliness

Her **effervescence** was contagious; she made everyone around her happy.

Questions

Q169

VISAGE

*Your Own Answer*_____

Q170

COFFER

*Your Own Answer*_____

Q171

VENERATE

*Your Own Answer*_____

Correct Answers

A169

n.—appearance; face

The artist's **visage** was often included in her paintings.

A170

n.—a chest where money or valuables are kept

The **coffer** that contained the jewels was stolen.

A171

v.—to revere

The missionary was **venerated** for the help he had given the homeless.

Questions

Q172

EPIGRAM

*Your Own Answer*_____

Q173

SWATHE

*Your Own Answer*_____

Q174

CAJOLE

*Your Own Answer*_____

Correct Answers

A172

n.—a witty or satirical poem or statement

The poet wrote an **epigram** about the upcoming election.

A173

v.—to wrap around something; to envelop

Soft blankets **swathe** the newborn baby.

A174

v.—to coax with insincere talk

To **cajole** the disgruntled employee, the manager coaxed him with lies and sweet talk.

Questions

Q175

BLATANT

*Your Own Answer*_____

Q176

MARAUDER

*Your Own Answer*_____

Q177

EXPLICIT

*Your Own Answer*_____

Correct Answers

A175

adj.—obvious; unmistakable; crude; vulgar

The **blatant** foul was reason for ejection.

A176

n.—plunderer or raider

The **marauder** had been traveling for two months searching for the large stash.

A177

adj.—specific; definite

The **explicit** recipe gave directions for making a very complicated dessert.

Questions

Q178

IMBUE

*Your Own Answer*_____

Q179

TENACIOUS

*Your Own Answer*_____

Q180

EXEMPLARY

*Your Own Answer*_____

Correct Answers

A178

v.—to soak or stain; to permeate
The wound will **imbue** the shirt in blood.

A179

adj.—holding; persistent
With a **tenacious** grip, the man was finally able to pull the nail from the wall.

A180

adj.—serving as an example; outstanding
The honor student's **exemplary** behavior made him a role model to the younger children.

Questions

Q181

MAVERICK

*Your Own Answer*_____

Q182

DISSEMINATE

*Your Own Answer*_____

Q183

SUPERLATIVE

*Your Own Answer*_____

Correct Answers

A181

n.—a person who does not conform to the norm

The **maverick** drove a large truck as others were purchasing compact cars.

A182

v.—to circulate; to scatter

He was hired to **disseminate** newspapers to everyone in the town.

A183

adj.—of the highest kind or degree

The Golden Gate Bridge is a **superlative** example of civil engineering.

Questions

Q184

IMPRECATE

*Your Own Answer*_____

Q185

ELOQUENCE

*Your Own Answer*_____

Q186

ADEPT

*Your Own Answer*_____

Correct Answers

A184

v.—to pray for evil; to invoke a curse

A witch may **imprecate** an enemy with a curse of bad luck.

A185

n.—the ability to speak well

The speaker's **eloquence** was attributed to his articulate manner of speaking.

A186

adj.—skilled; practiced

The skilled craftsman was quite **adept** at creating beautiful vases and candleholders.

Questions

MALEDICTION

*Your Own Answer*_____

DREGS

*Your Own Answer*_____

TORPID

*Your Own Answer*_____

Correct Answers

A187

n.—putting a curse on someone; talking negatively about another

With the threat of a **malediction**, the man left the fortune teller's house.

A188

n.—unwanted part

The **dregs** of the meal were given to the family pet.

A189

adj.—being dormant; slow, sluggish

When we came upon the hibernating bear, it was in a **torpid** condition.

Questions

PROVIDENT

*Your Own Answer*_____

EFFIGY

*Your Own Answer*_____

SAPID

*Your Own Answer*_____

Correct Answers

A190

adj.—prudent; economical
It was **provident**, in his opinion, to wait and buy the new car when he was financially secure.

A191

n.—the image or likeness of a person
Demonstrators carried **effigies** of the dictator they wanted overthrown.

A192

adj.—having a pleasant taste
Yellow and blue icing covered the **sapid** pastry.

Questions

Q193

EFFRONTERY

*Your Own Answer*_____

Q194

PENITENT

*Your Own Answer*_____

Q195

OMNISCIENT

*Your Own Answer*_____

Correct Answers

A193

n.—arrogance

The **effrontery** of the young man was offensive.

A194

adj.—feeling sorry for what one has done

The burglar expressed his **penitent** feelings during his confession.

A195

adj.—having knowledge of all things

The future can be told by the **omniscient** woman.

Questions

CONCEDE

*Your Own Answer*_____

SPORADIC

*Your Own Answer*_____

IMMUNE

*Your Own Answer*_____

Correct Answers

v.—to acknowledge; to admit; to surrender; to abandon one's position

After much wrangling, he **conceded** that the minister had a point.

adj.—rarely occurring or appearing; intermittent

In the desert there is usually only **sporadic** rainfall.

adj.—exempt from or protected against something

Doesn't everybody wish to be **immune** from the common cold?

Questions

Q199

HAUGHTY

*Your Own Answer*_____

Q200

CONVERGE

*Your Own Answer*_____

Q201

REBUTTAL

*Your Own Answer*_____

Correct Answers

adj.—proud of oneself and scornful of others

The **haughty** ways she displayed her work turned off her peers.

v.—to move toward one point (opposite: to diverge)

It was obvious that an accident was going to occur as the onlookers watched the two cars **converge**.

n.—refutation

The lawyer's **rebuttal** to the prosecutor's remarks caused the judge to disallow certain evidence.

Questions

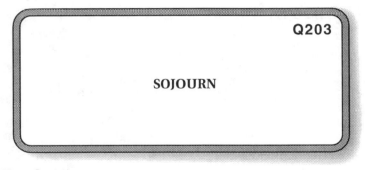

Q202

RANCID

Your Own Answer_____

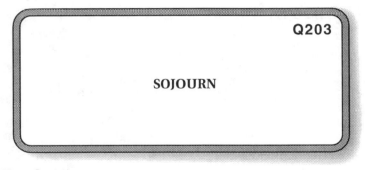

Q203

SOJOURN

Your Own Answer_____

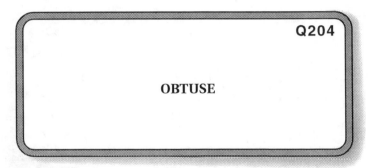

Q204

OBTUSE

Your Own Answer_____

Correct Answers

A202

adj.—having a bad odor or taste; rotten
Left out too long, the meat turned **rancid**.

A203

v.—to stay temporarily
The family will **sojourn** at their summer home.

A204

adj.—dull; greater than 90° but less than 180°; slow to understand or perceive
The man was so **obtuse**, he even made the dog yawn.

Questions

Q205

IMPUDENT

*Your Own Answer*_____

Q206

MUSE

*Your Own Answer*_____

Q207

HYPOTHETICAL

*Your Own Answer*_____

Correct Answers

A205

adj.—disrespectful and shameless
Impudent actions caused him to be unpopular.

A206

v.—to think or speak meditatively
I expect I'll have to **muse** on that question for a while.

A207

adj.—assumed; uncertain; conjectural
A **hypothetical** situation was set up so we could practice our responses.

Questions

Q208

PELLUCID

*Your Own Answer*_____

_____

Q209

EULOGY

*Your Own Answer*_____

_____

Q210

ULTERIOR

*Your Own Answer*_____

_____

Correct Answers

A208

adj.—transparent
The **pellucid** material was not an adequate shield from the sun.

A209

n.—words of praise, especially for the dead
The **eulogy** was a remembrance of the good things the man accomplished in his lifetime.

A210

adj.—remote; concealed; undisclosed
She was usually very selfish, so when she came bearing gifts he suspected that she had **ulterior** motives.

Questions

Q211

PROVOKE

*Your Own Answer*_____

_____

Q212

FLACCID

*Your Own Answer*_____

_____

Q213

BAUBLE

*Your Own Answer*_____

_____

Correct Answers

A211

v.—to stir to action or feeling; to arouse
By calling him names, he was **provoking** a fight.

A212

adj.—lacking firmness
The old dog's **flaccid** tail refused to wag.

A213

n.—a showy yet useless thing
The woman had many **baubles** on her book-
shelf.

Questions

Q214

DISPERSE

*Your Own Answer*_____

Q215

SPLENETIC

*Your Own Answer*_____

Q216

CYNIC

*Your Own Answer*_____

Correct Answers

A214

v.—to scatter; to separate

The pilots **dispersed** the food drops over a wide area of devastation.

A215

adj.—marked by hostility

The **splenetic** warriors advanced with no thought of what they were destroying.

A216

n.—one who believes that others are motivated entirely by selfishness

The **cynic** felt that the hero saved the man to become famous.

Questions

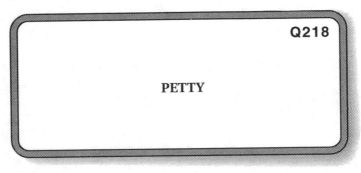

Q217

VITRIOLIC

*Your Own Answer*_____

Q218

PETTY

*Your Own Answer*_____

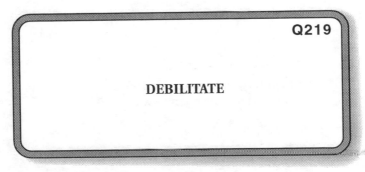

Q219

DEBILITATE

*Your Own Answer*_____

Correct Answers

A217

adj.—bitter

He was **vitriolic** after the confrontation.

A218

adj.—unimportant; of subordinate standing

With all of the crime in the world, stealing bubble gum is considered **petty** theft.

A219

v.—to enfeeble; to wear out

The phlebitis **debilitated** him to the point where he was unable even to walk.

Questions

Q220

SAGA

*Your Own Answer*_____

_____

Q221

IGNOMINIOUS

*Your Own Answer*_____

_____

Q222

BOMBASTIC

*Your Own Answer*_____

_____

Correct Answers

A220

n.—a legend; any long story of adventure or heroic deed

The **saga** of King Arthur and his court has been told for generations.

A221

adj.—contemptible; disgraced; degrading

The behavior was so **ignominious** he was ashamed to be associated with it.

A222

adj.—pompous; wordy; turgid

The **bombastic** woman talks a lot about herself.

Questions

Q223

CARTE BLANCHE

*Your Own Answer*_____

Q224

VIVACIOUS

*Your Own Answer*_____

Q225

PRATE

*Your Own Answer*_____

Correct Answers

A223

n.—unlimited authority

The designer was given **carte blanche** to create a new line for the fall.

A224

adj.—animated; gay

He is a great storyteller; his **vivacious** manner makes the tale come to life.

A225

v.—to talk to foolishly; to chatter

It is not uncommon for people to **prate** when they become nervous about speaking to a superior.

Questions

EVASION

*Your Own Answer*_____

STYMIE

*Your Own Answer*_____

CONTEMPT

*Your Own Answer*_____

Correct Answers

n.—the avoiding of a duty

The company was charged with tax **evasion**, as they did not pay all that they owed.

v.—to hinder or obstruct

Large amounts of snowfall will **stymie** the rescue effort.

n.—scorn; disrespect

The greedy, selfish banker was often discussed with great **contempt**.

Questions

Q229

DEPRECATE

*Your Own Answer*_____

Q230

DEPREDATION

*Your Own Answer*_____

Q231

CORROBORATE

*Your Own Answer*_____

Correct Answers

A229

v.—to express disapproval of; to protest against

The environmentalists **deprecated** the paper companies for cutting down ancient forests.

A230

n.—a plundering or laying waste

The pharaoh's once rich tomb was empty after centuries of **depredation** from grave robbers.

A231

v.—to confirm the validity of

The witness must **corroborate** the prisoner's story if she is to be set free.

Questions

Q232

FOIBLE

*Your Own Answer*_____

Q233

OMINOUS ✓

*Your Own Answer*_____

Q234

QUAINT ✓

*Your Own Answer*_____

Correct Answers

A232

n.—a minor weakness of character

My major **foible** is an inability to resist chocolate.

A233

adj.—threatening

Seeing ominous clouds on the horizon, the street fair organizers decided to fold up their tent and go home.

A234

adj.—old-fashioned; unusual; odd

One of the best qualities of the bed-and-breakfast was its **quaint** setting in the charming English village.

Questions

Q235

TEMPER ✓

*Your Own Answer*_____

Q236

VEX ✓

*Your Own Answer*_____

Q237

✓

CHERISH

*Your Own Answer*_____

Correct Answers

v.—to moderate, as by mingling with something else; to bring to the proper condition by treatment

She drew a hot bath, but then realized she'd have to **temper** it with a little cool water or end up scalded.

v.—to trouble the nerves; to annoy

He was beginning to **vex** her by asking a question every time she passed his locker.

v.—to feel love for

The bride vowed to **cherish** the groom for life.

Questions

Q238

TAUT

Your Own Answer (adj) stretched tightly.

Q239

DALLY

Your Own Answer (v) to waste time (loiter)

Q240

ABSOLVE

Your Own Answer (v) to forgive

Correct Answers

A238

adj.—stretched tightly; tense; extremely nervous

They knew a fish was biting, because the line suddenly became **taut**.

A239

v.—to loiter; to waste time

Please do not **dally** or we will miss our appointment.

A240

v.—to forgive; to acquit

The judge will **absolve** the person of all charges.

Questions

Q241

XENOPHOBIA

*Your Own Answer*_____

Q242

ATROPHY

*Your Own Answer*_____

Q243

REND

*Your Own Answer*_____

Correct Answers

A241

n.—fear of foreigners

Xenophobia kept the townspeople from encouraging any immigrants to move into the neighborhood.

A242

v.; n.—1. to waste away, as from lack of use; to wither 2. failure to grow

1. A few months after he lost his ability to walk, his legs began to **atrophy**.

2. The **atrophy** of the muscles was due to the injury.

A243

v.—to rip or pull from; to split with violence; to disturb with a sharp noise

When he saw the headlines, he wanted to **rend** the newspaper from his friend's hands.

Questions

Q244

UNDERMINE

*Your Own Answer*_____

Q245

CODDLE

*Your Own Answer*_____

Q246

PITHY

*Your Own Answer*_____

Correct Answers

A244

v.—to weaken, often through subtle means
The attempts to **undermine** the merger were unsuccessful.

A245

v.—to treat with tenderness
A baby needs to be **coddled**.

A246

adj.—terse and full of meaning
Columnist William Safire, a former presidential speechwriter, has a way with words that often yields **pithy** comments.

Questions

PAEAN

*Your Own Answer*_____

THWART

*Your Own Answer*_____

OUST

*Your Own Answer*_____

Correct Answers

A247

n.—a song of praise or triumph

A **paean** was written in honor of the victorious warrior.

A248

v.—to prevent from accomplishing a purpose; to frustrate

Their attempt to take over the country was **thwarted** by the palace guard.

A249

v.—to drive out; to eject

The dictator was **ousted** in a coup d'état.

Questions

Q250

FALLACIOUS

*Your Own Answer*_____

Q251

ALTERCATION

*Your Own Answer*_____

Q252

SCANTY

*Your Own Answer*_____

Correct Answers

A250

adj.—misleading

A used car salesman provided **fallacious** information that caused the naive man to purchase the old, broken car.

A251

n.—controversy; dispute

A serious **altercation** caused the marriage to end in a bitter divorce.

A252

adj.—inadequate; sparse

The malnutrition was caused by the **scanty** amount of healthy food eaten each day.

Questions

Q253

PARSIMONY

*Your Own Answer*_____

_____

Q254

CHASTE

*Your Own Answer*_____

_____

Q255

MUNIFICENT

*Your Own Answer*_____

_____

Correct Answers

A253

n.—to be unreasonably careful when spending

The **parsimony** of the wealthy woman was uncalled for.

A254

adj.—virtuous; free of obscenity

Because the woman believed in being **chaste**, she would not let her date into the house.

A255

adj.—giving generously

The civic group made a **munificent** donation to the homeless shelter.

Questions

Q256

LITIGATE

*Your Own Answer*_____

Q257

RAMIFICATION

*Your Own Answer*_____

Q258

ARDUOUS

*Your Own Answer*_____

Correct Answers

A256

v.—to carry on a lawsuit

A number of the state attorneys-general are **litigating** against the tobacco companies.

A257

n.—the arrangement of branches; consequence

One of the **ramifications** of driving fast is getting a speeding ticket.

A258

adj.—laborious, difficult; strenuous

Completing the plans for the new building proved to be an **arduous** affair.

Questions

Q259

SEQUESTER

*Your Own Answer*_____

Q260

CONSTRAIN

*Your Own Answer*_____

Q261

EXHUME

*Your Own Answer*_____

Correct Answers

v.—to separate or segregate
The jury was **sequestered** at the local inn.

v.—to force, compel; to restrain
It may be necessary to **constrain** the wild animal if it approaches the town.

v.—to unearth; to reveal
The scientists **exhumed** the body from the grave to test the body's DNA.

Questions

SYLLOGISM

*Your Own Answer*_____

_____

ABSCOND

*Your Own Answer*_____

_____

QUINTESSENCE

*Your Own Answer*_____

_____

Correct Answers

A262

n.—reasoning in order from general to particular

The **syllogism** went from fish to guppies.

A263

v.—to go away hastily or secretly; to hide

The newlywed couple will **abscond** from the reception to leave on the honeymoon.

A264

n.—the pure essence of anything

This story is the **quintessence** of American fiction.

Questions

MOTILITY

*Your Own Answer*_____

FALLIBLE

*Your Own Answer*_____

CONTEST

*Your Own Answer*_____

Correct Answers

A265

n.—spontaneous motion

The **motility** of the car caused the driver to lunge for the brake.

A266

adj.—liable to be mistaken or erroneous

By not differentiating themselves from the popular band, the group was especially **fallible**.

A267

v.—to disprove or invalidate

I will attempt to **contest** the criminal charges against me.

Questions

SINUOUS

*Your Own Answer*_____

TRAVAIL

*Your Own Answer*_____

AWRY

*Your Own Answer*_____

Correct Answers

A268

adj.—full of curves; twisting and turning

Sinuous mountain roads present extra danger at night when it's harder to see the road's edge.

A269

n.—very hard work; intense pain or agony

The farmer was tired after the **travail** of plowing the fields.

A270

adv.; adj.—1. crooked(ly); uneven(ly)
2. wrong; askew

1. Hearing the explosion in the laboratory, the scientist realized the experiment had gone **awry**.
2. The three-headed sheep was the result of an **awry** genetic experiment.

Questions

Q271

PROSELYTIZE

*Your Own Answer*_____

Q272

INCORPOREAL

*Your Own Answer*_____

Q273

BELITTLE

*Your Own Answer*_____

Correct Answers

A271

v.—to convert from one belief or religion to another

The preacher often attempts to **proselytize** wayward travelers.

A272

adj.—not consisting of matter

The apparition appeared to be **incorporeal**.

A273

v.—to make small; to think lightly of

The unsympathetic friend **belittled** her friend's problems and spoke of her own as the most important.

Questions

Q274

TYRANNY

*Your Own Answer*_____

Q275

FACADE

*Your Own Answer*_____

Q276

APPEASE

*Your Own Answer*_____

Correct Answers

A274

n.—absolute power; autocracy

The people were upset because they had no voice in the government that the king ran as a **tyranny**.

A275

n.—false appearance; front view of a building

The smile on her face was only a **facade** for her true feelings of sorrow.

A276

v.—to satisfy; to calm

A milk bottle usually **appeases** a crying baby.

Questions

CONDESCEND

*Your Own Answer*_____

DESPOIL

*Your Own Answer*_____

AGHAST

*Your Own Answer*_____

Correct Answers

A277

v.—to come down from one's position or dignity

The arrogant, rich man was usually **condescending** towards his servants.

A278

v.—to take everything; to plunder

The Huns **despoiled** village after village.

A279

adj.—astonished; amazed; horrified; terrified; appalled

Stockholders were **aghast** at the company's revelation.

Questions

WOODEN

*Your Own Answer*_____

STIGMA

*Your Own Answer*_____

IMPALE

*Your Own Answer*_____

Correct Answers

A280

adj.—to be expressionless or dull; made of wood; stiff

The **wooden** expression of the man made him look like a statue.

A281

n.—a mark of disgrace

The "F" on his transcript is a **stigma** on his record.

A282

v.—to pierce through with, or stick on, something pointed

The knight was **impaled** by the sharp lance.

Questions

Q283

OSCILLATE

*Your Own Answer*_____

Q284

IMPUGN

*Your Own Answer*_____

Q285

FLAG

*Your Own Answer*_____

Correct Answers

A283

v.—to move back and forth; to have a wavering opinion

The **oscillating** sprinkler system covered the entire lawn.

A284

v.—to attack with words; to question the truthfulness or integrity of

The defense lawyer **impugned** the witness's testimony, which set back the prosecution's case.

A285

v.—to become weak; to send a message

The smaller animal **flagged** before the larger one.

Questions

Q286

BLIGHT

*Your Own Answer*_____

Q287

AMBIVALENT

*Your Own Answer*_____

Q288

RENEGADE

*Your Own Answer*_____

Correct Answers

A286

n.; v.—1. a condition that kills plants; any person or thing that prevents growth 2. to cause destruction; to wither

1. The **blight** wiped out the entire corn crop.
2. The tornado **blighted** the entire town.

A287

adj.—undecided

The **ambivalent** jury could not reach a unanimous verdict.

A288

n.— a person who abandons something, as a religion, cause or movement; a traitor

Benedict Arnold remains one of the most notorious **renegades** in American history.

Questions

Q289

MELANCHOLY

*Your Own Answer*_____

Q290

WRY

*Your Own Answer*_____

Q291

PERVASIVE

*Your Own Answer*_____

Correct Answers

A289

n.— depression; gloom

The funeral parlor was filled with the **melancholy** of mourning.

A290

adj.—mocking; cynical

He has a **wry** sense of humor that sometimes hurts people's feelings.

A291

adj.—spreading throughout

The home was filled with the **pervasive** aroma of baking bread.

Questions

Q292

CONCLAVE

*Your Own Answer*_____

Q203

PERTINENT

*Your Own Answer*_____

Q294

QUALM

*Your Own Answer*_____

Correct Answers

A292

n.— any private meeting or closed assembly

The **conclave** was to meet in the executive suite.

A293

adj.—related to the matter at hand

During a trial everyone should concentrate on the same subject, stating only **pertinent** information.

A294

n.—sudden feeling of uneasiness or doubt

His **qualms** about flying disappeared once the plane landed softly.

Questions

PERJURY

*Your Own Answer*_____

_____

SURREPTITIOUS

*Your Own Answer*_____

_____

COHERENT

*Your Own Answer*_____

_____

Correct Answers

A295

n.—the voluntary violation of an oath or vow; false swearing

The already sensational trial of a star athlete turned all the more so when it turned out that a police detective had committed **perjury**.

A296

adj.—done secretly

The **surreptitious** maneuvers gave the advancing army an advantage.

A297

adj.—sticking together; connected; logical; consistent

The course was a success due to its **coherent** content.

Questions

Q298

EPICURE

*Your Own Answer*_____

Q299

AFFINITY

*Your Own Answer*_____

Q300

LAMENT

*Your Own Answer*_____

Correct Answers

n.—a person who has good taste in food and drink

As an **epicure**, Lance is choosy about the restaurants he visits.

n.—a connection; similarity of structure

There is a strong emotional **affinity** between the two siblings.

v.; n.—1. to mourn or grieve 2. expression of grief or sorrow

1. The boy is **lamenting** the loss of his pet.
2. The poem is a **lament** for his lost wife.

Questions

Q301

VENDETTA

*Your Own Answer*_____

_____

Q302

FORTUITOUS

*Your Own Answer*_____

_____

Q303

VILIFY

*Your Own Answer*_____

_____

Correct Answers

A301

n.—feud

The families' **vendetta** kept them off speaking terms for 50 years.

A302

adj.—happening accidentally

Finding the money under the bush was **fortuitous**.

A303

v.—to speak abusively of

The workers too often **vilify** an employer when upset with working conditions.

Questions

Q304

ADROIT

*Your Own Answer*_____

_____

Q305

DEPRAVITY

*Your Own Answer*_____

_____

Q306

PETULANT

*Your Own Answer*_____

_____

Correct Answers

A304

adj.—expert or skillful

The repair was not difficult for the **adroit** craftsman.

A305

n.—moral corruption; badness

Drugs and money caused **depravity** throughout the once decorous community.

A306

adj.—peevish; cranky; rude

The long illness put the boy in a **petulant** mood.

Questions

Q307

LAMBASTE

*Your Own Answer*_____

Q308

VOLATILE

*Your Own Answer*_____

Q309

PROPITIATE

*Your Own Answer*_____

Correct Answers

A307

v.—to scold or beat harshly

If the boy broke the lamp his father will surely **lambaste** him.

A308

adj.—changeable; undependable; unstable

It was a **volatile** situation; no one was willing to bet how things would turn out.

A309

v.—to win the goodwill of

If I try my best I will hopefully **propitiate** my new supervisor.

Questions

Q310

INSINUATE

*Your Own Answer*_____

Q311

LAUD

*Your Own Answer*_____

Q312

ADAMANT

*Your Own Answer*_____

Correct Answers

v.—to work into gradually and indirectly

He will **insinuate** his need for a vacation by saying how tired he has been lately.

v.; n.—1. to praise 2. a song or hymn of praise

1. He **lauded** his daughter for winning the trophy.
2. They sang a **laud** to the creator.

adj.—not yielding, firm

After taking an **adamant** stand to sell the house, the man called the real estate agency.

Questions

Q313

STAGNANT

*Your Own Answer*_____

_____

Q314

REPROACH

*Your Own Answer*_____

_____

Q315

COALESCE

*Your Own Answer*_____

_____

Correct Answers

A313

adj.—motionless, uncirculating

The **stagnant** water in the puddle became infested with mosquito larvae.

A314

v.—to blame and thus make feel ashamed; to rebuke

The major **reproached** his troops for not following orders.

A315

v.—to grow together

The bride and groom **coalesced** their funds to increase their collateral.

Questions

Q316

LURID

*Your Own Answer*_____

Q317

CULPABLE

*Your Own Answer*_____

Q318

DECOROUS

*Your Own Answer*_____

Correct Answers

A316

adj.—glowing through haze; shocking, sensational

A **lurid** sun shone upon them as they watched the sun set on the beach.

A317

adj.—deserving blame; guilty

The convicted criminal still denies that he is **culpable** for the robbery.

A318

adj.—showing decorum; propriety, good taste

This movie provides **decorous** refuge from the violence and mayhem that permeates the latest crop of Hollywood films.

Questions

Q319

ALOOF

*Your Own Answer*_____

Q320

TEEM

*Your Own Answer*_____

Q321

COMPREHENSIVE

*Your Own Answer*_____

Correct Answers

A319

adj.—distant in interest; reserved; cool
Even though the new coworker was **aloof**, we
attempted to be friendly.

A320

v.—to be stocked to overflowing; to pour out;
to empty
The new plant seemed to **teem** with insects.

(abound) OR
(swarm)

A321

adj.—all-inclusive; complete; thorough
It's the only health facility around to offer
comprehensive care.

Questions

<u>BEGET</u>

*Your Own Answer*_____

_____

TYCOON

*Your Own Answer*_____

_____

DETERMINATE

*Your Own Answer*_____

_____

Correct Answers

v.—<u>to bring into being</u>
The king wished to **beget** a new heir.

---

n.—wealthy leader
The business tycoon prepared to buy his
fifteenth company.

---

adj.—having distinct limits
The new laws were very determinate as far as
what was allowed and what was not allowed.

Questions

Q325

PREDECESSOR

*Your Own Answer*_____

Q326

PROPENSITY

*Your Own Answer*_____

Q327

STRIDENCY

*Your Own Answer*_____

Correct Answers

A325

n.—one who has occupied an office before another

Although her **predecessor** did not accomplish any goals that would help the poor, the new mayor was confident that she could finally help those in need.

A326

n.—a natural tendency towards; bias
I have a **propensity** to talk too fast.

A327

n.—harshness or shrillness of sound
The **stridency** of the whistle hurt the dog's ears.

Questions

CRASS

*Your Own Answer*_____

AFFABLE

*Your Own Answer*_____

DOWDY

*Your Own Answer*_____

Correct Answers

A328

adj.—stupid or dull; insensitive; materialistic; gross

To make light of someone's weakness is **crass**.

A329

adj.—friendly; amiable; good-natured

Her **affable** puppy loved to play with children.

A330

adj.—shabby in appearance

The **dowdy** girl had no buttons on her coat and the seams were falling apart.

Questions

INDICT

*Your Own Answer*_____

WAN

*Your Own Answer*_____

RENASCENCE

*Your Own Answer*_____

Correct Answers

A331

v.—to charge with a crime

The grand jury **indicted** her and her husband for embezzlement and six other lesser counts.

A332

adj.—lacking color; sickly pale

Her face became **wan** at the sight of blood.

A333

n.—a new life; rebirth

The **renascence** of the band resulted in a new recording contract.

Questions

Q334

PREVALENT

*Your Own Answer*_____

Q335

MELLIFLUOUS

*Your Own Answer*_____

Q336

CONFOUND

*Your Own Answer*_____

Correct Answers

A334

adj.—generally occurring

Rain is usually more **prevalent** than snow during April.

A335

adj.—having a sweet sound

The flute had a beautifully **mellifluous** sound.

A336

v.—to lump together, causing confusion; to damn

The problem **confounded** our ability to solve it.

Questions

Q337

PLACID

*Your Own Answer*_____

Q338

PHILANTHROPY

*Your Own Answer*_____

Q339

TENET

*Your Own Answer*_____

Correct Answers

A337

adj.—undisturbed and calm
The **placid** lake's water was completely motion-less.

A338

n.—charity; unselfishness
After years of donating time and money to the children's hospital, Mrs. Elderwood was commended for her **philanthropy**.

A339

n.—a principle accepted as authoritative
The **tenets** of socialism were explained in the book.

Questions

Q340

SYMMETRY

*Your Own Answer*_____

Q341

STANZA

*Your Own Answer*_____

Q342

OBSCURE

*Your Own Answer*_____

Correct Answers

A340

n.—correspondence of parts; harmony

The Roman columns give the building **symmetry**.

A341

n.—group of lines in a poem having a definite pattern

The poet uses an odd simile in the second **stanza** of the poem.

A342

adj.—not easily understood; dark

The orchestra enjoys performing **obscure** American works, hoping to bring them to a wider audience.

Questions

Q343

EBULLIENCE

*Your Own Answer*_____

Q344

SUMPTUOUS

*Your Own Answer*_____

Q345

IMPROMPTU

*Your Own Answer*_____

Correct Answers

A343

n.—an overflowing of high spirits; effervescence

She emanated **ebullience** as she skipped and sang down the hallway after learning of her promotion.

A344

adj.—involving great expense

A **sumptuous** spread of meats, vegetables, soups, and breads was prepared for the guests.

A345

adj.—without preparation ,

Her **impromptu** speech was well-received, giving her new confidence in her ability to speak off the cuff.

Questions

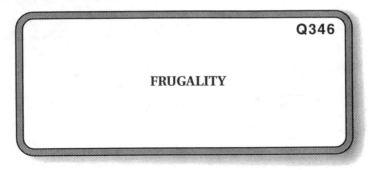

Q346

FRUGALITY

*Your Own Answer*_____

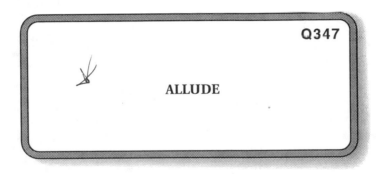

Q347

ALLUDE

*Your Own Answer*_____

Q348

RACONTEUR

*Your Own Answer*_____

Correct Answers

A346

n.—thrift; economical use or expenditure

His **frugality** limited him to purchasing the item for which he had a coupon.

A347

(v.)—to refer indirectly to something

The story **alludes** to part of the author's life.

A348

n.—a person skilled at telling stories

Our entertainment was a **raconteur** who told a story of talking animals.

Questions

Q349

✓

CHAGRIN

*Your Own Answer*_____

Q350

MALEFACTOR

*Your Own Answer*_____

Q351

CONNIVANCE

*Your Own Answer*_____

Correct Answers

A349

n.—a feeling of embarrassment due to failure or disappointment

To the **chagrin** of the inventor, the machine did not work.

A350

n.—an evil person

The **malefactor** ordered everyone to work over the holidays.

A351

n—secret cooperation in wrongdoing

With the guard's **connivance**, the convict was able to make his escape.

Questions

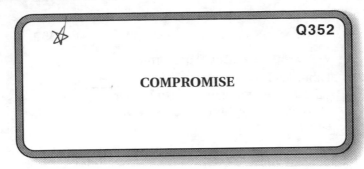

Q352

COMPROMISE

*Your Own Answer*_____

Q353

THROE

*Your Own Answer*_____

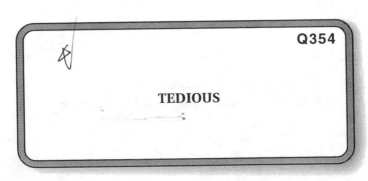

Q354

TEDIOUS

*Your Own Answer*_____

Correct Answers

A352

v.—to settle by mutual adjustment

Labor leaders and the automakers **compromised** by agreeing to a starting wage of $16 an hour in exchange for concessions on health-care premiums.

A353

n.—spasm or pang; agony

A particularly violent **throe** knocked her off her feet.

A354

adj.—wearisome, tiresome

Cleaning the house is a **tedious** chore for some people.

Questions

Q355

TRACTABLE

*Your Own Answer*_____

Q356

ELLIPSIS

*Your Own Answer*_____

Q357

COGITATE (?)

*Your Own Answer*_____

Correct Answers

A355

adj.—easily managed (opposite: intractable)
The boat was so lightweight it was **tractable** by
one person.

A356

n.—omission of words that would make the
meaning clear
The accidental **ellipsis** confused all those who
heard the speech.

A357

v.—to think hard; to ponder; to meditate
It is necessary to **cogitate** on decisions that
affect life goals.

cogitate

Questions

Q358

ABROGATE

*Your Own Answer*_____

Q359

ALLEGORY

*Your Own Answer*_____

Q360

SUCCINCT

*Your Own Answer*_____

Correct Answers

A358

v.—to cancel by authority ,

The judge would not **abrogate** the law.

A359

n.—a symbolic description

The book contained many **allegories** on Russian history.

A360

adj.—clearly stated; characterized by conciseness

The speech was **succinct** yet emotional.

Questions

JOCUND

*Your Own Answer*_____

DEBONAIR

*Your Own Answer*_____

HUBRIS

*Your Own Answer*_____

Correct Answers

A361

adj.—happy, cheerful, genial, gay

The puppy kept a smile on the **jocund** boy's face.

A362

adj.—having an affable manner; carefree; genial; suave

Opening the door for another is a **debonair** action.

A363

n.—arrogance

Some think it was **hubris** that brought the president to the point of impeachment.

Questions

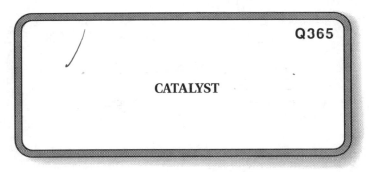

Q364

ABRIDGE

*Your Own Answer*_____

Q365

CATALYST

*Your Own Answer*_____

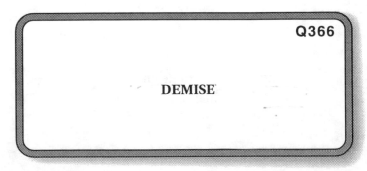

Q366

DEMISE

*Your Own Answer*_____

Correct Answers

A364

v.—to shorten; to limit

The editor **abridged** the story to make the book easier to digest.

A365

n.—anything that creates a situation in which change can occur

The low pressure system was the **catalyst** for the nor'easter.

A366

n.—ceasing to exist, as in death

The **demise** of Gimbels followed years of decline.

Questions

Q367

HAPLESS

*Your Own Answer*_____

Q368

AMALGAMATE

*Your Own Answer*_____

Q369

LEVITY

*Your Own Answer*_____

Correct Answers

A367

adj.—unlucky; unfortunate
The **hapless** team could not win a game.

A368

v.—to mix, merge, combine
If the economy does not grow, the business
may need to **amalgamate** with a rival company.

A369

n.—lack of seriousness; (instability)
The **levity** with which he faced the destruction
hampered the rescue effort.

Questions

Q370

DANK
‾‾‾‾

*Your Own Answer*_____

Q371

✓

FICKLE

*Your Own Answer*_____

Q372

✓

EXONERATE

*Your Own Answer*_____

Correct Answers

A370

adj.—damp and chilly
The cellar became very **dank** during the winter-time.

A371

adj.—changeable; unpredictable
He is quite fickle; just because he wants something today does not mean he will want it tomorrow.

A372

v.—to declare or prove blameless
Hopefully, the judge will **exonerate** you of any wrongdoing.

Questions

AGRARIAN

*Your Own Answer*_____

SEETHE

*Your Own Answer*_____

ANARCHIST

*Your Own Answer*_____

Correct Answers

A373

adj.—of the land; of or relating to farming

An **agrarian** economy relies primarily on farming.

A374

v.—to be violently disturbed

By the time I arrived, she was **seething** with anger.

A375

n.—one who believes that a formal government is unnecessary

The yell from the crowd came from the **anarchist** protesting the government.

Questions

Q376

TURBULENCE

*Your Own Answer*_____

Q377

PIOUS

*Your Own Answer*_____

Q378

OBDURATE

*Your Own Answer*_____

Correct Answers

A376

n.—condition of being physically agitated; disturbance

Everyone on the plane had to fasten their seatbelts as the plane entered an area of **turbulence**.

A377

adj.—religious; devout; dedicated

The religious couple believed that their **pious** method of worship would bring them eternal life.

A378

adj.—stubborn

The **obdurate** child refused to go to school.

Questions

ALLUSION

*Your Own Answer*_____

EVOKE

*Your Own Answer*_____

ARBITER

*Your Own Answer*_____

Correct Answers

n.—an indirect reference (often literary); a hint
The mention of the pet snake was an **allusion** to
the man's sneaky ways.

v.—to call forth; to provoke
Seeing her only daughter get married **evoked**
tears of happiness from the mother.

n.—one who is authorized to judge or decide
The decision of who would represent the
people was made by the **arbiter.**

Questions

Q382

FUSTIAN

*Your Own Answer*_____

Q383

PECCADILLO

*Your Own Answer*_____

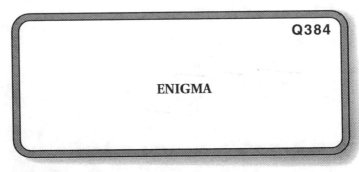

Q384

ENIGMA

*Your Own Answer*_____

Correct Answers

A382

n.—pompous talk or writing

The **fustian** by the professor made him appear arrogant.

A383

n.—a slight fault or offense

The child was embarrassed when he was caught committing the **peccadillo** of eating chocolate before dinner.

A384

n.—mystery; secret; perplexity

To all of the searchers, the missing child's location remained a great **enigma**.

Questions

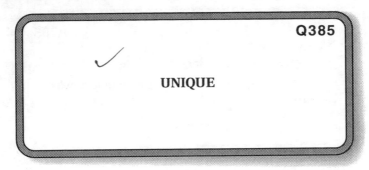

Q385

UNIQUE

*Your Own Answer*_____

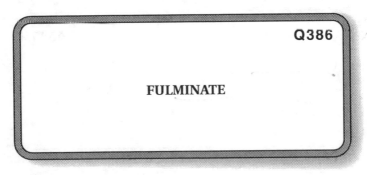

Q386

FULMINATE

*Your Own Answer*_____

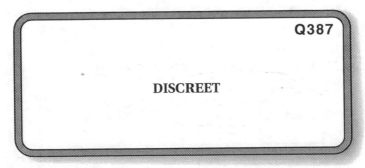

Q387

DISCREET

*Your Own Answer*_____

Correct Answers

A385

adj.—without equal; incomparable

The jeweler assured him that the necklace was **unique**, as it was part of a long-lost treasure.

A386

v.—to blame; to denounce

It is impolite to **fulminate** someone for your mistakes.

A387

adj.—showing good judgment in conduct; prudent

We confided our secret in Mary because we knew she'd be **discreet**.

Questions

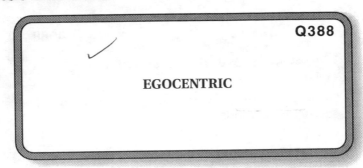

Q388

EGOCENTRIC

Your Own Answer_____

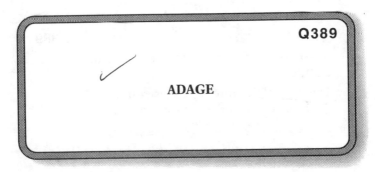

Q389

ADAGE

Your Own Answer_____

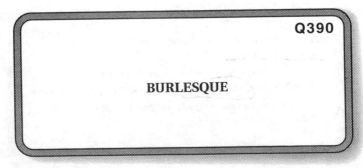

Q390

BURLESQUE

Your Own Answer_____

Correct Answers

adj.—self-centered, viewing everything in relation to oneself

The **egocentric** professor could not accept the students' opinions as valid.

n.—an old saying now accepted as being truthful

The **adage** "Do unto others as you wish them to do unto you" is still widely practiced.

v.; n.—1. to imitate in a nonserious manner 2. a comical imitation

1. His stump speeches were so hackneyed, he seemed to be **burlesquing** his role as a congressman.

2. George Burns was considered one of the great practitioners of **burlesque**.

Questions

Q391

LANGUID

*Your Own Answer*_____

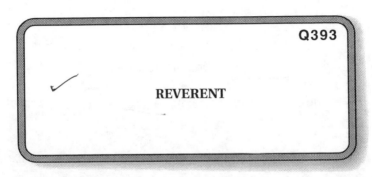

Q392

GREGARIOUS

*Your Own Answer*_____

Q393

REVERENT

*Your Own Answer*_____

Correct Answers

adj.—lacking vitality; indifferent
The **languid** student was always late to class.

adj.—fond of the company of others
Gregarious people may find those jobs with human contact more enjoyable than jobs that isolate them from the public.

adj.—respectful; feeling or showing deep love, respect, or awe

The congregation was very **reverent** of its spiritual leader.

Questions

QUAGMIRE

*Your Own Answer*_____

CONSUMMATION

*Your Own Answer*_____

PUTREFACTION

*Your Own Answer*_____

Correct Answers

A394

(n.)—marshy land; a difficult situation
The vehicle became stuck in the **quagmire**.

A395

(n.)—the completion; finish
Following the **consummation** of final exams,
most of the students graduated.

A396

(n.)—a mass of decomposed organic matter
The jack-o'-lantern was reduced to **putrefaction** by Thanksgiving.

Questions

Q397

COLLABORATE

*Your Own Answer*_____

Q398

NOXIOUS

*Your Own Answer*_____

Q399

ZENITH

*Your Own Answer*_____

Correct Answers

A397

(v.) – to work together; to cooperate

The two builders **collaborated** to get the house finished.

A398

(adj.) – harmful to one's health

The **noxious** fumes caused the person to become ill.

A399

(n.) – point directly overhead in the sky; highest point

The astronomer pointed her telescope straight up toward the **zenith**.

Questions

Q400

PALPABLE

*Your Own Answer*_____

Q401

INNOCUOUS

*Your Own Answer*_____

Q402

UNTOWARD

*Your Own Answer*_____

Correct Answers

A400

adj.—touchable; clear, obvious

The **palpable** decision was to discontinue the use of drugs.

A401

adj.—harmless; dull; innocent

The remark was rude but **innocuous**.

A402

adj.—improper; unfortunate

Asking guests to bring their own food would be an **untoward** request.

Questions

Q403

BLASPHEMOUS

*Your Own Answer*_____

Q404

LIBERALISM

*Your Own Answer*_____

Q405

DISAPPROBATION

*Your Own Answer*_____

Correct Answers

A403

adj.—irreligious; away from acceptable standards; speaking ill or using profane language.

The upper-class parents thought that it was **blasphemous** for their son to marry a waitress.

A404

n.—believing in personal freedom (favoring reform or progress)

If you believe in **liberalism,** the First Amendment is sacrosanct.

very holy

A405

n.—disapproval

Her **disapprobation** of her daughter's fiancé divided the family.

Questions

Q406

CHASTISE

*Your Own Answer*_____

Q407

BODE

*Your Own Answer*_____

Q408

FETID

*Your Own Answer*_____

Correct Answers

A406

v. - to punish; to discipline; to admonish

The dean (chastised) the first-year student for cheating on the exam.

A407

v. - to foretell something

The storm **bode** that we would not reach our destination.

A408

adj. - having a smell of decay

The **fetid** smell led us to believe something was decaying in the basement.

Questions

PRISTINE

*Your Own Answer*_____

PARIAH

*Your Own Answer*_____

JESTER

*Your Own Answer*_____

Correct Answers

A409

adj.—primitive, pure, uncorrupted
The **pristine** lake had not been marred by pollution.

A410

n.—an outcast
The **pariah** of the group sat by himself under the tree.

A411

n.—a person employed to amuse
The **jester** tried all of his tricks to get the girl to laugh.

Questions

Q412

DOGGEREL

*Your Own Answer*_____

Q413

GUFFAW

*Your Own Answer*_____

Q414

SYNTHETIC

*Your Own Answer*_____

Correct Answers

A412

n.—verse characterized by <u>forced rhyme</u> and meter

Contrary to its appearance, a **doggerel** can contain some weighty messages.

---

rough, noisy, lively

A413

n.—<u>boisterous laughter</u>

A comedian's success is <u>assured</u> when the audience gives forth a **guffaw** following his jokes.

A414

adj.—not real, rather artificial

The **synthetic** skin was made of a thin rubber.

Questions

Q415

TERRESTRIAL

*Your Own Answer*_____

Q416

SUBJUGATE

*Your Own Answer*_____

Q417

ITINERARY

*Your Own Answer*_____

Correct Answers

A415

adj.—pertaining to the earth
Deer are **terrestrial** animals; fish are aquatic.

A416

v.—to dominate or enslave
The bully will attempt to **subjugate** the remainder of the class.

A417

n.—travel plan; schedule; course
Their trip's **itinerary** was disrupted by an unexpected snowstorm.

Questions

Q418

HACKNEYED

*Your Own Answer*_____

Q419

YORE

*Your Own Answer*_____

Q420

SCURRILOUS

*Your Own Answer*_____

Correct Answers

A418

adj.—commonplace; trite

Just when you thought neckties were becoming a **hackneyed** gift item, along comes the Grateful Dead collection.

A419

n.—former period of time

When he sees his childhood friends, they speak about the days of **yore**.

A420

adj.—vulgar

The **scurrilous** language made the mother twinge.

Questions

Q421

PALINDROME

*Your Own Answer*_____

Q422

AUTOCRAT

*Your Own Answer*_____

Q423

FINESSE

*Your Own Answer*_____

Correct Answers

A421

n.—a word or phrase that reads the same backwards and forwards

Bob, Dad, and Madam are examples of **palindromes**.

A422

n.—an absolute ruler

The **autocrat** in charge of the government was a man of power and prestige.

A423

n.—the ability to handle situations with skill and diplomacy

The executive with the most **finesse** was chosen to meet with the diplomats.

Questions

Q424

BURLY

*Your Own Answer*_____

Q425

JUXTAPOSE

*Your Own Answer*_____

Q426

CASTIGATE

*Your Own Answer*_____

Correct Answers

A424

adj.—strong; bulky; stocky
The lumberjack was a **burly** man.

A425

v.—to place side-by-side
The author decided to **juxtapose** the two sentences since they each strengthened the meaning of the other.

A426

v.—to punish through public criticism
The mayor **castigated** the police chief for the rash of robberies.

Questions

Q427

GNARLED

*Your Own Answer*_____

_____

Q428

PAINSTAKING

*Your Own Answer*_____

_____

Q429

RABID

*Your Own Answer*_____

_____

Correct Answers

A427

adj.—full of knots; twisted

The raven perched in the **gnarled** branches of the ancient tree.

A428

adj.—thorough, careful, precise

Helga's **painstaking** research paid off with a top grade on her essay.

A429

adj.—furious; with extreme anger; affected with the disease called rabies

The insult made him **rabid**.

Questions

Q430

KITH

*Your Own Answer*_____

Q431

VOLITION

*Your Own Answer*_____

Q432

SALVAGE

*Your Own Answer*_____

Correct Answers

A430

n.—relatives and acquaintances
Our **kith** will meet at the family reunion.

A431

n.—the act of making a choice or decision
He attended the meeting of his own **volition**.

A432

n.; v.—1. the rescue or saving of any
property or goods from destruction
2. to rescue from loss

1. The **salvage** of the ship brought up thousands
of gold coins.
2. The family tried to **salvage** their belongings
after their home was destroyed by a tornado.

Questions

Q433

CURSORY

*Your Own Answer*_____

Q434

EUPHONY

*Your Own Answer*_____

Q435

DEROGATORY

*Your Own Answer*_____

Correct Answers

A433

adj.—hasty; slight

The detective's **cursory** examination of the crime scene caused him to overlook the lesser clues.

A434

n.—pleasant combination of sounds

The gently singing birds created a beautiful **euphony.**

A435

adj.—belittling; uncomplimentary

He was upset because his annual review was full of **derogatory** comments.

Questions

TENTATIVE

*Your Own Answer*_____

_____

ODIOUS

*Your Own Answer*_____

_____

WANTON

*Your Own Answer*_____

_____

Correct Answers

adj.—not confirmed; indefinite

Not knowing if he'd be able to get the days off, Al went ahead anyway and made **tentative** vacation plans with his pal.

adj.—hateful; disgusting

Having to chaperone her brother was an **odious** chore for the girl.

adj.—unmanageable; unjustifiably malicious

My **wanton** hunger must be satiated.

Questions

MIMICRY

*Your Own Answer*_____

MIEN

*Your Own Answer*_____

OBSOLETE

*Your Own Answer*_____

Correct Answers

n.—imitation

The comedian's **mimicry** of the president's gestures had the audience rolling in the aisles.

n.—appearance, being, or manner

Her **mien** was typically one of distress, especially after the mishap.

adj.—out-of-date; passé

Computers have made many formerly manual tasks **obsolete**.

Questions

CHOLERIC

*Your Own Answer*_____

PALLIATE

*Your Own Answer*_____

EPITOME

*Your Own Answer*_____

Correct Answers

A442

adj.—cranky; cantankerous; easily moved to feeling displeasure

The **choleric** man was continually upset by his neighbors.

A443

v.—to alleviate or ease pain but not cure; to make appear less serious

The medication will help **palliate** the pain.

A444

n.—model; typification; representation

The woman chosen to lead the dancers was the **epitome** of true grace.

Questions

Q445

INSUBORDINATE

*Your Own Answer*_____

Q446

NEUTRAL

*Your Own Answer*_____

Q447

WORKADAY

*Your Own Answer*_____

Correct Answers

A445

adj.—disobedient to authority

The boy's **insubordinate** behavior was a constant source of tension between the school and his parents.

A446

adj.—impartial; unbiased

The mother remained **neutral** regarding the argument between her two children.

A447

adj.—commonplace

The **workaday** meal was not exciting to the world-class chef.

Questions

Q448

ERRANT

*Your Own Answer*_____

Q449

NASCENT

*Your Own Answer*_____

Q450

EXECUTE

*Your Own Answer*_____

Correct Answers

A448

adj.—roving in search of adventure

The young man set out across country on an **errant** expedition.

A449

adj.—starting to grow or develop

The **nascent** rage of in-line skating began on the West Coast.

A450

v.—to put to death; to kill; to carry out; to fulfill

The evil, murderous man was **executed** for killing several innocent children.

Questions

Q451

INNOVATE

*Your Own Answer*_____

_____

Q452

PRECIPITATE

*Your Own Answer*_____

_____

Q453

MERCENARY

*Your Own Answer*_____

_____

Correct Answers

---

v.—to introduce a change; to depart from the old

She **innovated** a new product for the home construction market.

---

v.; adj.—1. to cause to happen; happening quickly 2. falling steeply; quick

1. A rude comment may **precipitate** an argument.

2. The **precipitate** flood caught the village off-guard.

---

adj.; n.—1. working or done for payment only 2. hired soldier

1. Lila was suspicious that Joe had jumped at the chance only for **mercenary** reasons.

2. A **mercenary** was hired for a hundred dollars a month, good money in those days even if you had to fight a war to get it.

Questions

Q454

HOARY

Your Own Answer_____

Q455

FRENETIC

Your Own Answer_____

Q456

ARCHETYPE

Your Own Answer_____

Correct Answers

A454

adj.—whitened by age

The paint had a **hoary** appearance, as if it were applied decades ago.

A455

adj.—frenzied

A **frenetic** call was made from the crime scene.

A456

n.—original pattern or model; prototype

This man was the **archetype** for scores of fictional characters.

Questions

Q457

DOGMATIC

*Your Own Answer*_____

Q458

CRAVEN

*Your Own Answer*_____

Q459

CONSTERNATION

*Your Own Answer*_____

Correct Answers

A457

adj.—stubborn; biased; opinionated
Their **dogmatic** declaration clarified their position.

A458

n.; adj.—1. coward; abject person 2. cowardly
1. While many fought for their rights, the **craven** sat shaking off in a corner somewhere.
2. **Craven** men will not stand up for what they believe in.

A459

n.—amazement or terror that causes confusion
The look of **consternation** on the child's face caused her father to panic.

Questions

CONVIVIALITY

*Your Own Answer*_____

RUMINATE

*Your Own Answer*_____

GRANDIOSE

*Your Own Answer*_____

Correct Answers

A460

n.—a fondness for festiveness or joviality

His **conviviality** makes him a welcome guest at any social gathering.

A461

v.—to consider carefully

The doctor will **ruminate** on his diagnosis.

A462

adj.—magnificent; flamboyant

His **grandiose** idea was to rent a plane to fly to Las Vegas for the night.

Questions

Q463

BIASED

*Your Own Answer*_____

Q464

APPROBATORY

*Your Own Answer*_____

Q465

LACERATE

*Your Own Answer*_____

Correct Answers

A463

adj.—prejudiced; influenced; not neutral

The vegetarian had a **biased** opinion regarding what should be ordered for dinner.

A464

adj.—approving or sanctioning

The judge showed his acceptance in his **approbatory** remark.

A465

v.—to tear or mangle; to wound or hurt

Sharp knives may **lacerate** the skin of an unsuspecting user.

Questions

Q466

RESCIND

*Your Own Answer*_____

Q467

BASTION

*Your Own Answer*_____

Q468

LUSTROUS

*Your Own Answer*_____

Correct Answers

A466

v.—to retract; to discard; to revoke, repeal, or cancel

Sensing that the intent of the regulation had long ago been realized, the city agency **rescinded** the order.

A467

n.—a fortified place or strong defense

The strength of the **bastion** saved the soldiers inside of it.

A468

adj.—bright; radiant; shining

Surrounded by rubies, the **lustrous** diamond looked magnificent.

Questions

Q469

AMBIGUOUS

*Your Own Answer*_____

_____

Q470

PORTEND

*Your Own Answer*_____

_____

Q471

ANTIPATHY

*Your Own Answer*_____

_____

Correct Answers

A469

adj.—not clear; uncertain; vague

The **ambiguous** law did not make a clear distinction between the new and old land boundary.

A470

v.—to be an omen of; to signify

The distant roll of thunder **portends** an oncoming storm.

A471

n.—a strong dislike or repugnance

Her **antipathy** for large crowds convinced her to decline the invitation to the city.

Questions

Q472

ATTENUATE

*Your Own Answer*_____

Q473

INFER

*Your Own Answer*_____

Q474

REFUTE

*Your Own Answer*_____

Correct Answers

A472

v.—to thin out; to weaken

Water is commonly used to **attenuate** strong chemicals.

A473

v.—form an opinion; to conclude

From the broad outline he supplied it was easy to **infer** that the applicant knew a great deal about trains.

A474

v.—to challenge; to disprove

He **refuted** the proposal, deeming it unfair.

Questions

INFAMOUS

*Your Own Answer*_____

WRETCHED

*Your Own Answer*_____

INDIGNANT

*Your Own Answer*_____

Correct Answers

A475

adj.—having a bad reputation; notorious

After producing machines that developed many problems, the production company became **infamous** for poor manufacturing.

A476

adj.—miserable or unhappy; causing distress

Brought up in an orphanage, Annie led a **wretched** existence.

A477

adj.—expressing anger over an injustice

He was **indignant** over the way he was treated.

Questions

Q478

ACCLAIM

*Your Own Answer*_____

Q479

BENEFACTOR

*Your Own Answer*_____

Q480

EXULTATION

*Your Own Answer*_____

Correct Answers

A478

n.—loud approval; applause

Edward Albee's brilliantly written Broadway revival of *A Delicate Balance* received wide **acclaim**.

A479

n.—one who helps others; a donor

An anonymous **benefactor** donated $10,000 to the children's hospital.

A480

n.—the act of rejoicing

Exultation was evident by the partying and revelry.

Questions

Q481

EXTRANEOUS

*Your Own Answer*_____

Q482

REITERATE

*Your Own Answer*_____

Q483

PERCEPTIVE

*Your Own Answer*_____

Correct Answers

A481

adj.—irrelevant; not related; not essential

Discussing the long, boring lecture, most people agreed that much of the information was **extraneous**.

A482

v.—to repeat again

Rose found that she had to **reiterate** almost everything, leading her to fear her husband was going deaf.

A483

adj.—full of insight; aware

The **perceptive** detective discovered that the murder weapon was hidden in a safe under the floor.

Questions

Q484

ASSUAGE

Your Own Answer_____

Q485

INGENIOUS

Your Own Answer_____

Q486

CONGLOMERATION

Your Own Answer_____

Correct Answers

A484

v.—to relieve; to ease; to make less severe
Medication should **assuage** the pain.

A485

adj.—clever, resourceful
His **ingenious** idea made it possible to double
production at no extra cost.

A486

n.—a collection or mixture of various things
The **conglomeration** is made up of four different interest groups.

Questions

Q487

SUNDER

*Your Own Answer*_____

Q488

RESIGNATION

*Your Own Answer*_____

Q489

KEN

*Your Own Answer*_____

Correct Answers

A487

v.—to break; to split in two
The Civil War threatened to **sunder** the United States.

A488

n.—quitting; submission
He submitted his **resignation** because he found a new job.

A489

v.; n.—1. to recognize 2. one's understanding
1. It was difficult to **ken** exactly what she had in mind.
2. My **ken** of the situation proved to be incorrect.

Questions

PURVIEW

*Your Own Answer*_____

_____

HERESY

*Your Own Answer*_____

_____

PECUNIARY

*Your Own Answer*_____

_____

Correct Answers

A490

n.—the extent of something

His actions were within the **purview** of the law.

A491

n.—opinion contrary to popular belief

In this town it is considered **heresy** to want parking spaces to have meters.

A492

adj.—pertaining to money

The retiring employee was delighted when he received a **pecuniary** gift.

Questions

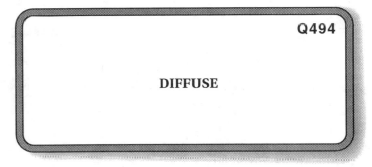

Q493

MACERATE

*Your Own Answer*_____

Q494

DIFFUSE

*Your Own Answer*_____

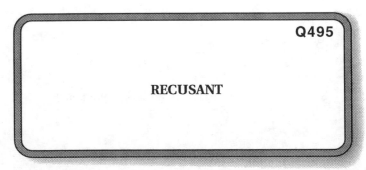

Q495

RECUSANT

*Your Own Answer*_____

Correct Answers

A493

v.—to soften by steeping in liquid

It was necessary to **macerate** the food before the elderly man could eat it.

A494

adj.—spread out; verbose (wordy); not focused

The toys were discovered in a **diffuse** manner after the birthday party.

A495

adj.—disobedient of authority

Recusant inmates may be denied privileges.

Questions

Q496

HYPERBOLE

*Your Own Answer*_____

Q497

KNOTTY

*Your Own Answer*_____

Q498

ADDLED

*Your Own Answer*_____

Correct Answers

A496

n.—an exaggeration, not to be taken seriously

The full moon was almost blinding in its brightness, he said with a measure of **hyperbole**.

A497

adj.—to be puzzling or hard to explain

The mystery was **knotty**.

A498

adj.—rotten; confused

The egg will become **addled** if it is left unrefrigerated.

Questions

Q499

VIRULENT

*Your Own Answer*_____

Q500

MALINGER

*Your Own Answer*_____

Q501

PHOBIA

*Your Own Answer*_____

Correct Answers

A499

adj.—deadly; harmful; malicious
Rattlesnakes use a **virulent** poison to kill their prey.

A500

v.—to pretend to be ill in order to escape work
He is known to **malinger** on Fridays in order to have a three-day weekend.

A501

n.—morbid fear
Fear of heights is a not uncommon **phobia**.

Questions

Q502

PARLEY

*Your Own Answer*_____

Q503

VENAL

*Your Own Answer*_____

Q504

RECLUSE

*Your Own Answer*_____

Correct Answers

A502

v.—to speak with another; to discourse

I will **parley** the information to the appropriate person.

A503

adj.—can be readily bribed or corrupted

Venal employees caused the downfall of the company.

A504

adj.; n.—1. solitary 2. a person who lives secluded

1. His **recluse** life seems to make him happy.

2. Howard Hughes, among the most famous and enigmatic figures of the 20th century, ultimately retreated to a life as a **recluse**.

Questions

Q505

RAUCOUS

*Your Own Answer*_____

_____

Q506

CALLOW

*Your Own Answer*_____

_____

Q507

ABYSMAL

*Your Own Answer*_____

_____

Correct Answers

A505

adj.—disagreeable to the sense of hearing; harsh; hoarse

The **raucous** protesters stayed on the street corner all night, shouting their disdain for the whale killers.

A506

adj.—being young or immature

With the **callow** remark the young man demonstrated his age.

A507

adj.—very deep; absolutely wretched

The **abysmal** waters contained little plant life.

Questions

Q508

ZEALOT

*Your Own Answer*_____

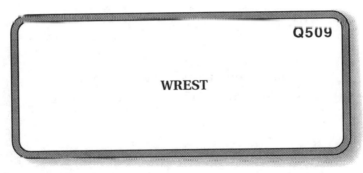

Q509

WREST

*Your Own Answer*_____

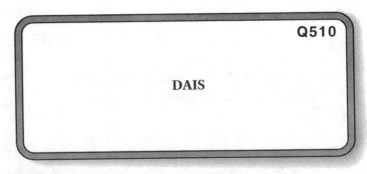

Q510

DAIS

*Your Own Answer*_____

Correct Answers

A508

n.—believer; enthusiast; fan
The **zealot** followed whatever rules the cult leader set.

A509

v.—to pull or force away by a violent twisting
The warriors **wrested** the power from the king.

A510

n.—a raised platform at one end of a room
The **dais** was raised to make the speaker look taller.

Questions

CAPRICE

*Your Own Answer*_____

METICULOUS

*Your Own Answer*_____

WHIMSICAL

*Your Own Answer*_____

Correct Answers

A511

n.—a sudden, unpredictable, or whimsical change

The **caprice** with which the couple changed their plans demonstrated to their young age.

A512

adj.—exacting; precise

The lab technicians must be **meticulous** in their measurements to obtain exact results.

A513

adj.—fanciful; subject to erratic behavior

Strolling down Disney World's Main Street is bound to put both children and adults in a **whimsical** mood.

Questions

Q514

ASCETIC

*Your Own Answer*_____

Q515

JARGON

*Your Own Answer*_____

Q516

PENSIVE

*Your Own Answer*_____

Correct Answers

A514

n.; adj.—1. one who leads a simple life of self-denial 2. rigorously abstinent

1. The monastery is filled with **ascetics** who have devoted their lives to religion.
2. The nuns lead an **ascetic** life devoted to the Lord.

A515

n.—incoherent speech; specialized vocabulary in certain fields

The conversation was nothing but **jargon**, but then the speakers were nothing but cartoon characters who specialize in an oddly bracing form of gibberish.

A516

adj.—reflective; contemplative

She was in a **pensive** mood, just wanting to be alone to think.

Questions

Q517

VENEER

*Your Own Answer*_____

Q518

FERVOR

*Your Own Answer*_____

Q519

DIN

*Your Own Answer*_____

Correct Answers

A517

n.—a thin surface layer; any attractive but superficial appearance

The wood color **veneer** was peeling off the counter.

A518

n.—passion; intensity of feeling

The crowd was full of **fervor** as the candidate entered the hall.

A519

n.—a noise that is loud and continuous

The **din** of the jackhammers reverberated throughout the concrete canyon.

Questions

Q520

OBTRUDE

*Your Own Answer*_____

Q521

IMPERTURBABLE

*Your Own Answer*_____

Q522

PREFATORY

*Your Own Answer*_____

Correct Answers

A520

v.—to force oneself or one's ideas upon another; to thrust forward; to eject

The inquisitive coworker **obtrudes** into the conversation often.

A521

adj.—calm; not easily excited

The **imperturbable** West Point graduate made a fine negotiator.

A522

adj.—coming before

The **prefatory** comments informed the audience of what was to come.

Questions

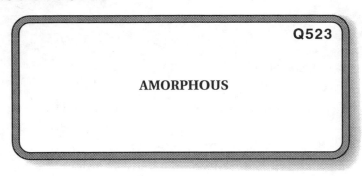

Q523

AMORPHOUS

*Your Own Answer*_____

_____

Q524

HEED

*Your Own Answer*_____

_____

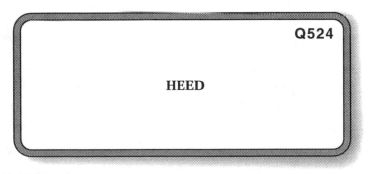

Q525

CHARISMA

*Your Own Answer*_____

_____

Correct Answers

A523

adj.—with no shape; unorganized; having no determinate form

The **amorphous** gel seeped through the cracks.

A524

v.—to obey; to yield to

If the peasant **heeds** the king's commands, he will be able to keep his land.

A525

n.—appeal; magnetism; presence

She has such **charisma** that everyone likes her the first time they meet her.

Questions

Q526

INARTICULATE

*Your Own Answer*_____

_____

Q527

MANDATE

*Your Own Answer*_____

_____

Q528

PERIPHERAL

*Your Own Answer*_____

_____

Correct Answers

A526

adj.—speechless; unable to speak clearly

He was so **inarticulate** that he had trouble making himself understood.

A527

n.—order; charge

The new manager wrote a **mandate** declaring that smoking was now prohibited in the office.

A528

adj.—marginal; outer

Those are **peripheral** problems; let's look at the central challenge.

Questions

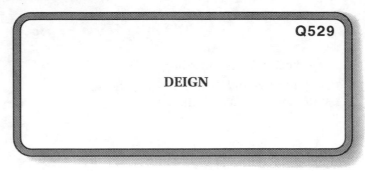

Q529

DEIGN

*Your Own Answer*_____

Q530

ARCANE

*Your Own Answer*_____

Q531

LOQUACIOUS

*Your Own Answer*_____

Correct Answers

v.—to condescend; to stoop

He said he wouldn't **deign** to dignify her statement with a response.

adj.—obscure; secret; mysterious

With an **arcane** expression, the young boy left the family wondering what sort of mischief he had committed.

adj.—very talkative; garrulous

She was having difficulty ending the conversation with her **loquacious** neighbor.

Questions

LEVEE

*Your Own Answer*_____

GERRYMANDER

*Your Own Answer*_____

BELLICOSE

*Your Own Answer*_____

Correct Answers

A532

n.—an embankment on the edge of a river or field; a reception held by a person of distinction

The swimmer came ashore on the **levee**.

A533

v.—to gain advantage by manipulating unfairly

To **gerrymander** during negotiations is considered unfair.

A534

adj.—quarrelsome; warlike

The **bellicose** guest would not be invited back again.

Questions

Q535

SURMISE

*Your Own Answer*_____

Q536

ERRATIC

*Your Own Answer*_____

Q537

ENCROACH

*Your Own Answer*_____

Correct Answers

A535

n.; v.—1. a guess 2. to guess
1. Was my **surmise** correct?
2. I **surmise** that we will not arrive at the party on time.

A536

adj.—unpredictable; irregular
His **erratic** behavior was attributed to the shocking news he had received.

A537

v.—to trespass or intrude
It is unlawful to **encroach** on another's private property.

Questions

Q538

TURPITUDE

*Your Own Answer*_____

Q539

LIAISON

*Your Own Answer*_____

Q540

OSSIFY

*Your Own Answer*_____

Correct Answers

n.—vileness

The **turpitude** of the action caused rage among the people.

n.—connection; link; illicit sexual relationship

The student council served as a **liaison** between the faculty and the student body.

v.—to turn to bone; to harden

Over time, the plant matter has **ossified**.

Questions

SOVEREIGN

*Your Own Answer*_____

MAUDLIN

*Your Own Answer*_____

EXTRAPOLATE

*Your Own Answer*_____

Correct Answers

A541

adj.—superior; supreme in power or rank; independent of others

The power was given to the **sovereign** warrior.

A542

adj.—foolishly and tearfully sentimental

The **maudlin** affair consisted of three speeches in honor of the benefactor.

A543

v.—to estimate the value of something beyond the scale; to infer what is unknown from something known

The budget for the next five years was **extrapolated** from that year's data.

Questions

INCORRIGIBLE

*Your Own Answer*_____

HARBOR

*Your Own Answer*_____

ASEPTIC

*Your Own Answer*_____

Correct Answers

A544

adj.—not capable of correction or improvement

The mischievous boy was an **incorrigible** practical joker.

A545

n.; v.—1. a place of safety or shelter 2. to give shelter or to protect

1. We stood at the dock as the ship sailed into the **harbor**.

2. The peasants were executed for **harboring** known rebels.

A546

adj.—germfree

It is necessary for an operating room to be **aseptic**.

Questions

Q547

DEBAUCHERY

*Your Own Answer*_____

Q548

GOURMAND

*Your Own Answer*_____

Q549

ANALOGY

*Your Own Answer*_____

Correct Answers

A547

n.—indulgence in one's appetites
The preacher decried **debauchery** and urged charity.

A548

n.—one who enjoys eating and drinking
A **gourmand** may eat several servings of an entree.

A549

n.—similarity; correlation; parallelism
The teacher used an **analogy** to describe the similarities between the two books.

Questions

Q550

FLUX

*Your Own Answer*_____

Q551

FLEDGLING

*Your Own Answer*_____

Q552

ELUSIVE

*Your Own Answer*_____

Correct Answers

A550

n.—a flow; a continual change

With the **flux** of new students into the school, space was limited.

A551

n.—inexperienced person; beginner

The **fledgling** mountain climber needed assistance from the more experienced mountaineers.

A552

adj.—hard to catch

Even the experienced, old fisherman admitted that the trout in the river were quite **elusive**.

Questions

Q553

IDIOSYNCRASY

*Your Own Answer*_____

Q554

JUNCTURE

*Your Own Answer*_____

Q555

UNFEIGNED

*Your Own Answer*_____

Correct Answers

A553

n.—any personal peculiarity, mannerism

Her tendency to bite her lip is an **idiosyncrasy**.

A554

n.—critical point; meeting

When the gas changed into a liquid, they sensed that they'd come to a critical **juncture** in their experimentation.

A555

adj.—genuine; real; sincere

Her **unfeigned** reaction of surprise meant she had not expected the party.

Questions

Q556

KNAVERY

*Your Own Answer*_____

Q557

LUCRATIVE

*Your Own Answer*_____

Q558

SUPPLANT

*Your Own Answer*_____

Correct Answers

A556

n.—a dishonest act
An act of **knavery** is cause for loss of trust.

A557

adj.—profitable; gainful
She entered the pharmaceutical industry in the belief that it would be **lucrative**.

A558

v.—to take the place of
Can you **supplant** me if I cannot play?

Questions

FIDELITY

*Your Own Answer*_____

LUXURIANT

*Your Own Answer*_____

ACERBIC

*Your Own Answer*_____

Correct Answers

A559

n.—faithfulness; honesty

His **fidelity** was proven when he turned in the lost money.

A560

adj.—growing with energy and in great abundance; magnificent

The **luxuriant** flowers grew in every available space.

A561

adj.—acid in temper, mood, or tone; sour in taste

Too much bay leaf will make the eggplant **acerbic**.

Questions

Q562

EQUIVOCATION

*Your Own Answer*_____

Q563

IMPASSIVE

*Your Own Answer*_____

Q564

ANONYMOUS

*Your Own Answer*_____

Correct Answers

A562

n.—a purposely misleading statement

The **equivocations** by the man sent the search team looking in the wrong direction.

A563

adj.—showing no emotion

Even when his father died he gave an **impassive** response and walked out tearless.

A564

adj.—nameless; unidentified

Not wishing to be identified by the police, he remained **anonymous** by returning the money he had stolen by sending it through the mail.

Questions

Q565

ESOTERIC

*Your Own Answer*_____

Q566

IDEOLOGY

*Your Own Answer*_____

Q567

INIQUITOUS

*Your Own Answer*_____

Correct Answers

A565

adj.—understood by only a chosen few; confidential

The **esoteric** language was known only by the select group.

A566

n.—creed; representative way of thinking

His **ideology** proved to be faulty.

A567

adj.—wicked; unjust

The verbal abuse towards the man was truly **iniquitous**.

Questions

Q568

DISSONANCE

*Your Own Answer*_____

Q569

COMPLACENT

*Your Own Answer*_____

Q570

STRIDENT

*Your Own Answer*_____

Correct Answers

A568

n.—musical discord; a mingling of inharmonious sounds; nonmusical; disagreement; lack of harmony

Much twentieth-century music is not liked by classical music lovers because of the **dissonance** it holds and the harmonies it lacks.

A569

adj.—content; self-satisfied; smug

The CEO worries regularly that his firm's winning ways will make it **complacent**.

A570

adj.—creaking; harsh, grating

Her **strident** voice hampered her chances of getting the announcer position.

Questions

Q571

SUPPRESS

Your Own Answer

Q572

PROGENY

Your Own Answer

Q573

FANATIC

Your Own Answer

Correct Answers

A571

v.—to bring to an end; to hold back
The illegal aliens were **suppressed** by the border patrol.

A572

n.—children; offspring
It is through his **progeny** that his name shall live on.

A573

n.—enthusiast; extremist
The terrorist group, comprised of **fanatics**, wanted to destroy those who disagreed with them.

Questions

Q574

AMENDMENT

*Your Own Answer*_____

Q575

SUSCEPTIBLE

*Your Own Answer*_____

Q576

WARRANT

*Your Own Answer*_____

Correct Answers

A574

n.—a positive change

The **amendment** in his ways showed there was still reason for hope.

A575

adj.—easily imposed; inclined

She gets an annual flu shot since she is **susceptible** to becoming ill.

A576

n.; v.—1. authorization or sanction; a wrting serving as authorization for something 2. to justify; to authorize

1. The officer received the **warrant** to search the suspect's house.
2. The police official **warranted** the arrest of the suspect once enough proof had been found.

Questions

Q577

PERVADE

*Your Own Answer*_____

Q578

IRASCIBLE

*Your Own Answer*_____

Q579

ILLUSIVE

*Your Own Answer*_____

Correct Answers

A577

v.—to occupy the whole of
Her perfume was so strong that it **pervaded** the whole room.

A578

adj.—prone to anger
The **irascible** teenager was known to cause fights when upset.

A579

adj.—deceiving, misleading
It was as **illusive** as a mirage.

Questions

Q580

UNEQUIVOCAL

*Your Own Answer*_____

Q581

DESECRATE

Your Own Answer _____

Q582

TETHER

*Your Own Answer*_____

Correct Answers

A580

adj.—clear and unambiguous

The 50-0 vote against the bill was an **unequivocal** statement against the measure.

A581

v.—to profane; to violate the sanctity of

The teenagers' attempt to **desecrate** the church disturbed the community.

A582

n.; v.—1. a rope or chain to fasten an animal or object to keep it from wandering; the limit of one's ability 2. to fasten or confine

1. My **tether** of playing basketball is shooting air balls.
2. He **tethered** the horse to the post.

Questions

Q583

NEXUS

*Your Own Answer*_____

Q584

MOOT

*Your Own Answer*_____

Q585

DISCOURSE

*Your Own Answer*_____

Correct Answers

n.—a connection

The **nexus** between the shuttle and the space station was successful.

adj.—subject to or open for discussion or debate

The discussion of extending the girl's curfew was a **moot** point.

v.—to converse; to communicate in an orderly fashion

The scientists **discoursed** on a conference call for just five minutes but were able to solve three major problems.

Questions

Q586

NEGLIGENCE

*Your Own Answer*_____

Q587

LETHARGIC

*Your Own Answer*_____

Q588

HONE

*Your Own Answer*_____

Correct Answers

A586

n.—carelessness

Negligence contributed to the accident: she was traveling too fast for the icy conditions.

A587

adj.—lazy; passive

Feeling very **lethargic**, he watched television or slept the whole day.

A588

n.; v.—1. something used to sharpen 2. to sharpen; to long or yearn for

1. He ran the knife over the **hone** for hours to get a razor-sharp edge.

2. The apprenticeship will give her the opportunity to **hone** her skills.

Questions

Q589

ABSTRUSE

*Your Own Answer*_____

Q590

SAUNTER

*Your Own Answer*_____

Q591

BANEFUL

*Your Own Answer*_____

Correct Answers

A589

adj.—hard to understand; deep; recondite

The topic was so **abstruse** the student was forced to stop reading.

A590

v.—to walk at a leisurely pace; to stroll

The loving couple **sauntered** down the wooded path.

A591

adj.—deadly or causing distress, death

Not wearing a seatbelt could be **baneful**.

Questions

Q592

EVANESCENT

*Your Own Answer*_____

Q593

MISANTHROPE

*Your Own Answer*_____

Q594

NULLIFY

*Your Own Answer*_____

Correct Answers

A592

adj.—vanishing quickly; dissipating like a vapor

The **evanescent** mirage could be seen only at a certain angle.

A593

n.—a person who distrusts everything; a hater of mankind

After the man swindled all of the woman's savings, she became a **misanthrope**.

A594

v.—to cancel; to invalidate

Drinking alcohol excessively will **nullify** the positive benefits of eating well and exercising daily.

Questions

Q595

TRIBUTE

*Your Own Answer*_____

Q596

LICENTIOUS

*Your Own Answer*_____

Q597

BROACH

*Your Own Answer*_____

Correct Answers

A595

n.—expression of admiration

Her performance was a **tribute** to her retiring teacher.

A596

adj.—morally lacking in restraint

Historians say that **licentious** behavior led to the downfall of Rome.

A597

v.—to introduce into conversation

Broaching the touchy subject was difficult.

Questions

Q598

REPAST

*Your Own Answer*_____

Q599

PROVINCIAL

*Your Own Answer*_____

Q600

DIGRESS

*Your Own Answer*_____

Correct Answers

n.—food that is eaten

The **repast** consisted of cheese, wine, and bread.

adj.—regional; unsophisticated

After living in the city for five years, he found that his family back home on the farm was too **provincial** for his cultured ways.

v.—to stray from the subject; to wander from the topic

It is important to not **digress** from the plan of action.

Questions

Q601

EMINENCE

*Your Own Answer*_____

Q602

EFFLUVIUM

*Your Own Answer*_____

Q603

SCOURGE

*Your Own Answer*_____

Correct Answers

A601

n.—a lofty place; superiority

After toiling in the shadows for years, at last she achieved **eminence**.

A602

n.—an outflow of vapor of invisible particles; a noxious odor

The **effluvium** from the exhaust had a bad smell.

A603

v.; n.—1. to whip severely; to punish; to subject to affliction 2. any instrument used to inflict punishment; cause of serious trouble

1. The trainer will **scourge** the animal if it attacks someone.
2. The whip was the **scourge** that the lions learned to obey.

Questions

Q604

LABYRINTH

*Your Own Answer*_____

Q605

STATIC

*Your Own Answer*_____

Q606

INDIGENCE

*Your Own Answer*_____

Correct Answers

n.—maze

Be careful not to get lost in the **labyrinth** of vegetation.

adj.—inactive; changeless

The view while riding in the train across the endless, flat landscape remained **static** for days.

n.—the condition of being poor

The family's **indigence** was evident by the run-down house they lived in.

Questions

Correct Answers

A607

adj.; n.—1. adapted for obtaining a result; guided by self-interest 2. a means to an end; something used in an emergency.

1. The mayor chose the more **expedient** path rather than the more correct one.
2. The **expedient** is used when all else fails.

A608

adj.—shriveled; withered
The **wizened** face of the old man was covered by his hat.

A609

adj.—that which can be justified
A good strategy needs to be **defensible**.

Questions

Q610

SUAVE

*Your Own Answer*_____

Q611

VICISSITUDE

*Your Own Answer*_____

Q612

MISER

*Your Own Answer*_____

Correct Answers

A610

adj.—effortlessly gracious
She was a **suave** negotiator, always getting what she wanted without anyone feeling they'd lost anything.

A611

n.—unpredictable change occurring in life
They stayed married for over fifty years despite the **vicissitudes** of life.

A612

n.—penny-pincher, stingy person
The **miser** made no donations and loved counting his money every night.

Questions

Q613

STOKE

*Your Own Answer*_____

Q614

RIVET

*Your Own Answer*_____

Q615

MINUTE

*Your Own Answer*_____

Correct Answers

A613

v.—to feed fuel to, especially a fire

With the last embers dying, he **stoked** the fire one more time.

A614

v.; n.—1. to secure; to hold firmly, as in eyes 2. a belt used to hold plates or beams together

1. We can **rivet** the boat to the dock.
2. The **rivet** fell from the construction site and into the street.

A615

n.; adj.—1. sixty seconds; a short period of time
2. extremely small, tiny

1. The woman said she would only take a **minute** to pick out the items she wanted to buy.
2. Being on a sodium-restricted diet, he uses only a **minute** amount of salt in his dishes.

Questions

EXPUNGE

*Your Own Answer*_____

UNRULY

*Your Own Answer*_____

CONNOISSEUR

*Your Own Answer*_____

Correct Answers

v.—to blot out; to delete

The juvenile's record will be **expunged** when he turns the age of 18.

adj.—not submitting to discipline; disobedient

The **unruly** boys had to be removed from the concert hall.

n.—expert; authority (usually refers to a wine or food expert)

They allowed her to choose the wine for dinner since she was the **connoisseur**.

Questions

SHADY

*Your Own Answer*_____

OPULENCE

*Your Own Answer*_____

PREVARICATE

*Your Own Answer*_____

Correct Answers

A619

adj.—a character of questionable honesty

A **shady** person would not be trusted with a sensitive secret.

A620

n.—wealth; fortune

A 40-room mansion on 65 wooded acres is only the most visible sign of her **opulence**.

A621

v.—to speak equivocally or evasively, i.e., to lie

The mayor's desperate attempt to **prevaricate** about the scandal was transparent to the voters.

Questions

NAUTICAL

*Your Own Answer*_____

ABNEGATION

*Your Own Answer*_____

REPREHEND

*Your Own Answer*_____

Correct Answers

A622

adj.—of the sea; having to do with sailors, ships, or navigation

The coastal New England town had a charming **nautical** influence.

A623

n.—a denial

The woman's **abnegation** of her loss was apparent when she began to laugh.

A624

v.—to reprimand; to censure

The teacher **reprehended** the student in front of the class.

Questions

Q625

UBIQUITOUS

*Your Own Answer*_____

Q626

PEDANTIC

*Your Own Answer*_____

Q627

PERFUNCTORY

*Your Own Answer*_____

Correct Answers

A625

adj.—omnipresent; present everywhere

An **ubiquitous** spirit followed the man wherever he went.

A626

adj.—emphasizing minutiae or form in scholarship or teaching

Professor Jones's lectures were so **pedantic** that his students sometimes had a tough time understanding the big picture.

A627

adj.—done in a routine, mechanical way, without interest

Changing careers is a good cure for people who have become bored with their occupation and are currently performing their duties in a **perfunctory** fashion.

Questions

Q628

VERBIAGE

*Your Own Answer*_____

Q629

INHERENT

*Your Own Answer*_____

Q630

MITE

*Your Own Answer*_____

Correct Answers

n.—wordiness

I enjoy speeches that contain little **verbiage**.

adj.—part of the essential character; intrinsic

A constant smile is **inherent** in pageant competitors.

n.—a very small sum of money; very small creature; a small amount

The **mite** they pay me is hardly worth the aggravation.

Questions

Q631

SATURNINE

*Your Own Answer*_____

Q632

FERMENT

*Your Own Answer*_____

Q633

BEMUSE

*Your Own Answer*_____

Correct Answers

adj.—gloomy, sluggish; to cause or undergo fermentation

The never-ending rain put everyone in a **saturnine** mood.

v.—to excite or agitate

The rally cry was meant to **ferment** and confuse the opponent.

v.—to preoccupy in thought

The girl was **bemused** by her troubles.

Questions

Q634

EXCULPATE

*Your Own Answer*_____

Q635

CONTUSION

*Your Own Answer*_____

Q636

EPIPHANY

*Your Own Answer*_____

Correct Answers

A634

v.—to free from guilt

The therapy session will **exculpate** the man from his guilty feelings.

A635

n.—a bruise; an injury where the skin is not broken

The man was fortunate to receive only **contusions** from the crash.

A636

n.—an appearance of a supernatural being

The man bowed to the **epiphany**.

Questions

Q637

PONDEROUS

*Your Own Answer*_____

Q638

DAUNTLESS

*Your Own Answer*_____

Q639

VORACIOUS

*Your Own Answer*_____

Correct Answers

A637

adj.—unwieldy from weight; dull or labored

The **ponderous** piano posed a serious challenge to having it pulled up to the 16th floor.

A638

adj.—fearless; not discouraged

The **dauntless** ranger scaled the mountain to complete the rescue.

A639

adj.—greedy in eating

After not eating for two days the dog had a **voracious** appetite.

Questions

Correct Answer

Q640

ABASE

*Your Own Answer*_____

Q641

VISCOUS

*Your Own Answer*_____

Q642

FORMIDABLE

*Your Own Answer*_____

Correct Answers

abase **A640**

v.—to degrade; to humiliate; to disgrace
The mother's public reprimand **abased** the girl.

A641

adj.—thick and sticky (said of fluids)
The **viscous** honey poured slowly from the jar.

A642

adj.—something that causes dread or fear
The **formidable** team caused weak knees in the opponents.

Questions

Q643

TEMPERAMENT

*Your Own Answer*_____

Q644

FEIGN

*Your Own Answer*_____

Q645

IMPASSE

*Your Own Answer*_____

Correct Answers

A643

n.—one's customary frame of mind
The girl's **temperament** is usually very calm.

---

feign

A644

v.—to pretend
It is not uncommon for a child to **feign** illness in order to stay home from school.

A645

n.—a situation that has no solution or escape
The workers and administration were at an **impasse** in their negotiations.

Questions

Q646

BOMBAST

*Your Own Answer*_____

Q647

PLETHORA

*Your Own Answer*_____

Q648

SARDONIC

*Your Own Answer*_____

Correct Answers

A646

n.—pompous speech; pretentious words

After he delivered his **bombast** at the podium, he arrogantly left the meeting.

A647

n.—a superabundance

There was a **plethora** of food at the royal feast.

A648

adj.—having a sarcastic quality

H. L. Mencken was known for his **sardonic** writings on political figures.

Questions

COGNITIVE

*Your Own Answer*_____

TOXIC

*Your Own Answer*_____

CEREMONIOUS

*Your Own Answer*_____

Correct Answers

A649

adj.—possessing the power to think or meditate; meditative; capable of perception

Cognitive thought makes humans adaptable to a quickly changing environment.

A650

adj.—poisonous

It's best to store cleansing solutions out of children's reach because of their **toxic** contents.

A651

adj.—very formal or proper

The black-tie dinner was highly **ceremonious**.

Questions

Q652

APOCALYPTIC

*Your Own Answer*_____

Q653

VACILLATION

*Your Own Answer*_____

Q654

BUNGLER

*Your Own Answer*_____

Correct Answers

A652

adj.—pertaining to a discovery or new revelation; symbolizing the ultimate defeat of evil and triumph of good

Science-fiction movies seem to relish **apocalyptic** visions.

A653

n.—fluctuation

It was difficult to draw a conclusion from the experiments since there was so much **vacillation** in the results.

A654

n.—a clumsy person

The one who broke the crystal vase was a true **bungler**.

Questions

Q655

RIBALD

*Your Own Answer*_____

Q656

SURFEIT

*Your Own Answer*_____

Q657

GUISE

*Your Own Answer*_____

Correct Answers

A655

adj.—characterized by vulgar joking or mocking

Some people find the comedian's **ribald** act offensive.

A656

v.; n.—1. to excessively indulge 2. overindulgence

1. The teenagers were warned not to **surfeit** at the party.

2. The result of her **surfeit** was a week of regret.

A657

n.—appearance

The undercover detective, under the **guise** of friendship, offered to help the drug runner make a connection.

Questions

Q658

DELETERIOUS

*Your Own Answer*_____

Q659

VIGILANCE

*Your Own Answer*_____

Q660

PARRY

*Your Own Answer*_____

Correct Answers

A658

adj.—harmful; hurtful; noxious
Deleterious fumes escaped from the over-
turned truck.

A659

n.—watchfulness
The child could not escape the **vigilance** of his
mother's eyes.

A660

v.—to avoid; to ward off
I dislike talking to the woman so I will attempt
to **parry** her by ducking around the corner.

Questions

Q661

SLOVENLY

*Your Own Answer*_____

Q662

PEDAGOGUE

*Your Own Answer*_____

Q663

TRENCHANT

*Your Own Answer*_____

Correct Answers

adj.—sloppy in dress or person; carelessly done

His mother-in-law did not approve of his **slovenly** manner.

n.—a teacher

Seeing the way she worked with children there was no doubt she was a true **pedagogue**.

adj.—cutting; keen or incisive; forceful or vigorous

The doctor's **trenchant** orders were the one factor that saved the patient.

Questions

Q664

GRAVITY

Your Own Answer_____

Q665

BENEVOLENT

Your Own Answer_____

Q666

DEFAMATION

Your Own Answer_____

Correct Answers

A664

n.—seriousness

The **gravity** of the incident was sufficient to involve the police and the FBI.

A665

adj.—kind; generous

The professor proved a tough questioner, but a **benevolent** grader.

A666

n.—harm to a name or reputation; to slander

The carpenter felt that the notoriousness of his former partner caused **defamation** to his construction business.

Questions

Q667

JUDICIOUS

*Your Own Answer*_____

Q668

FATUOUS

*Your Own Answer*_____

Q669

IMMUTABLE

*Your Own Answer*_____

Correct Answers

A667

adj.—having or showing sound judgment
Because the elder was **judicious**, the tough decisions were left to him.

A668

adj.—lacking in seriousness; vain and silly
The **fatuous** prank was meant to add comedy to the situation.

A669

adj.—unchangeable; permanent
The ties that bind alumni to their university are **immutable**.

Questions

Q670

BURGEON

*Your Own Answer*_____

Q671

ABSTINENCE

*Your Own Answer*_____

Q672

DOCILE

*Your Own Answer*_____

Correct Answers

A670

v.—to grow or develop quickly

The tumor appeared to **burgeon** more quickly than normal.

A671

n.—the act or process of voluntarily refraining from any action or practice; self-control; chastity

In preparation for the Olympic games, the athletes practiced **abstinence** from red meat and junk food, adhering instead to a menu of pasta and produce.

A672

adj.—manageable; obedient; gentle

We needed to choose a **docile** pet because we hadn't the patience for a lot of training.

Questions

REPREHENSIBLE

*Your Own Answer*_____

CONTEMPORARY

*Your Own Answer*_____

SYCOPHANT

*Your Own Answer*_____

Correct Answers

A673

adj.—wicked; disgraceful
Slashing their tires was a **reprehensible** act.

A674

adj.—living or happening at the same time;
modern
Contemporary furniture will clash with your
traditional sectional.

A675

n.—flatterer
Rodolfo honed his skills as a **sycophant**, hoping
it would get him into Sylvia's good graces.

Questions

Q676

DORMANT

*Your Own Answer*_____

Q677

FRACTIOUS

*Your Own Answer*_____

Q678

RATIFY

*Your Own Answer*_____

Correct Answers

A676

adj.—as if asleep
The plants lay **dormant** until the spring thaw.

A677

adj.—rebellious; apt to quarrel
Fractious siblings aggravate their parents.

A678

v.—to make valid; to confirm
The Senate **ratified** the new law that would
prohibit companies from discriminating
according to race in their hiring practices.

Questions

Q679

CONNOTATIVE

*Your Own Answer*_____

Q680

DILETTANTE

*Your Own Answer*_____

Q681

VANTAGE

*Your Own Answer*_____

Correct Answers

A679

adj.—containing associated meanings in addition to the primary one

Along with the primary meaning of the word, there were two **connotative** meanings.

A680

n.—an admirer of the fine arts; a dabbler

Though she played the piano occasionally, she was more of a **dilettante**.

A681

n.—favorable position; position allowing a clear view or understanding

He was at a **vantage** point in his career, and expected to be promoted soon.

Questions

Q682

THRIFTY

*Your Own Answer*_____

Q683

DECADENCE

*Your Own Answer*_____

Q684

RECTIFY

*Your Own Answer*_____

Correct Answers

A682

adj.—frugal, careful with money

Being **thrifty**, the woman would not purchase the item without a coupon.

A683

n.—a decline in morals or art

Some believe the **decadence** of Nero's rule led to the fall of the Roman Empire.

A684

v.—to correct

The service manager **rectified** the shipping mistake by refunding the customer's money.

Questions

MALLEABLE

*Your Own Answer*_____

INSTIGATE

*Your Own Answer*_____

SEDITION

*Your Own Answer*_____

Correct Answers

A685

adj.—easy to shape or bend; pliable
The **malleable** material was formed into a "U" shape.

A686

v.—to start; to provoke
It was uncertain to the police as to which party **instigated** the riot.

A687

n.—a revolt
The **sedition** by the guards ended with their being executed for treason.

Questions

Q688

RESURGENT

*Your Own Answer*_____

Q689

PRATTLE

*Your Own Answer*_____

Q690

TRITE

*Your Own Answer*_____

Correct Answers

A688

adj.—rising or tending to rise again

A **resurgent** wave of enthusiasm erupted from the once quiet crowd.

A689

n.; v.—1. childish babble 2. to babble while speaking

1. I've listened to his **prattle** for far too long.

2. The toddler does more **prattling** than talking.

A690

adj.—commonplace; overused

The committee was looking for something new, not the same **trite** ideas.

Questions

Q691

OBEISANCE

*Your Own Answer*_____

Q692

AUTOCRACY

*Your Own Answer*_____

Q693

CAPTIOUS

*Your Own Answer*_____

Correct Answers

A691

n.—a gesture of respect or reverence

As an **obeisance**, the man took off his hat as the funeral procession drove past him.

A692

n.—an absolute monarchy; government where one person holds power

The **autocracy** was headed by a demanding man.

A693

adj.—disposed to find fault

A **captious** attitude often causes difficulties in a relationship.

Questions

INVOKE

*Your Own Answer*_____

PINIONED

*Your Own Answer*_____

CLANDESTINE

*Your Own Answer*_____

Correct Answers

A694

v.—to ask for; to call upon
The parishioners **invoked** divine help for their troubles.

A695

adj.—bound fast
The two rafts were **pinioned** by steel wire.

A696

adj.—secret
The **clandestine** plan must be kept between the two of us!

Questions

Q697

DECISIVENESS

*Your Own Answer*_____

Q698

ABERRANT

*Your Own Answer*_____

Q699

INIMICAL

*Your Own Answer*_____

Correct Answers

A697

n.—an act of being firm or determined
Decisiveness is one of the key qualities of a successful executive.

A698

adj.—abnormal; straying from the normal or usual path
The **aberrant** flight pattern of the airplane alarmed the air traffic controllers.

A699

adj.—hostile, unfriendly
The chess player directed an **inimical** stare at his opponent to knock him off his game.

Questions

Q700

ADVOCATE

*Your Own Answer*_____

Q701

DELINEATE

*Your Own Answer*_____

Q702

RUDIMENTARY

*Your Own Answer*_____

Correct Answers

A700

v.; n.—1. to plead in favor of 2. supporter; defender

1. Amnesty International **advocates** the cause of human rights.

2. Martin Luther King, Jr. was a great **advocate** of civil rights.

A701

v.—to outline; to describe

She **delineated** her plan so that everyone would have a basic understanding of it.

A702

adj.—elementary

Adding two plus two is a **rudimentary** activity.

BLANK CARDS
To Make Up
Your Own Questions

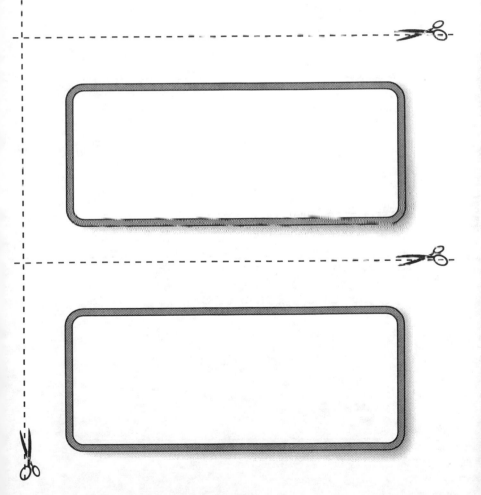

CORRECT ANSWERS

for

Your Own Questions

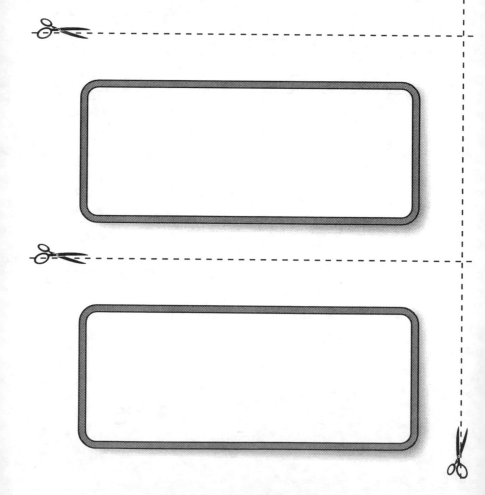

Blank Cards for
Your Own Questions

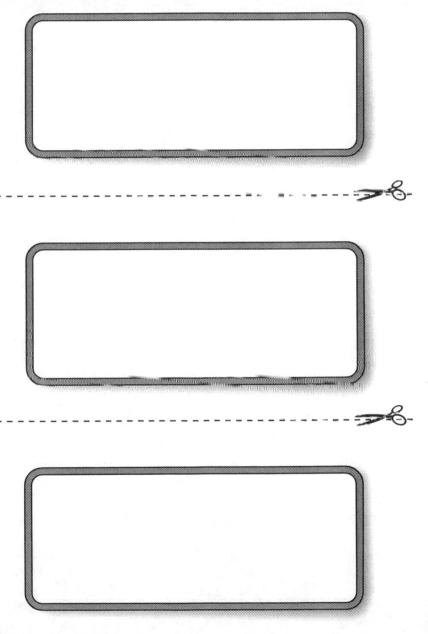

Correct Answers

Blank Cards for
Your Own Questions

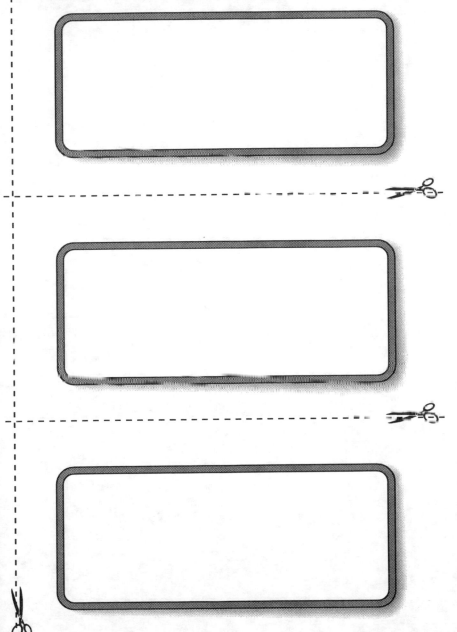

Correct Answers

Blank Cards for *Your Own Questions*

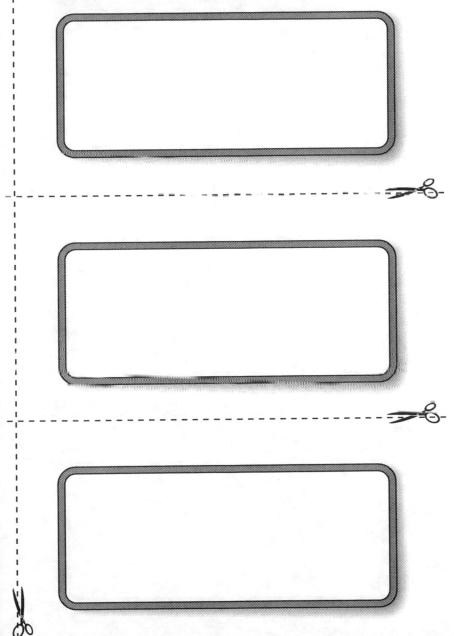

Correct Answers

Blank Cards for
Your Own Questions

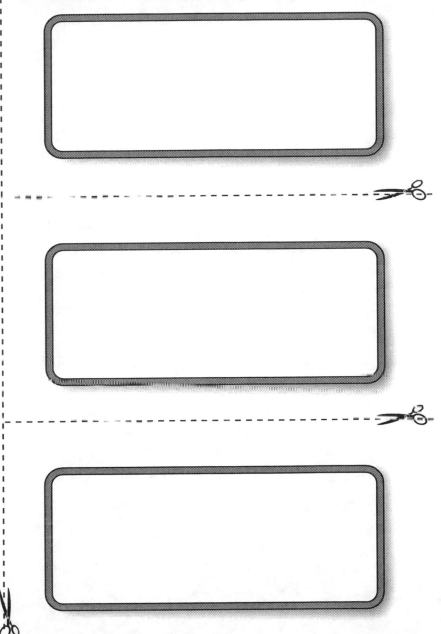

Correct Answers

Blank Cards for *Your Own Questions*

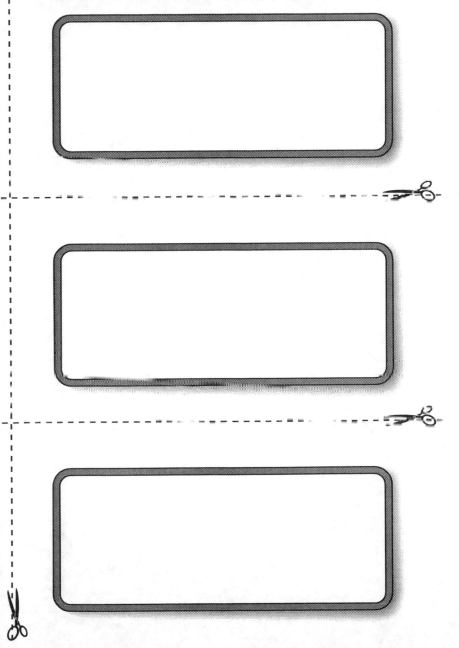

Correct Answers

Blank Cards for
Your Own Questions

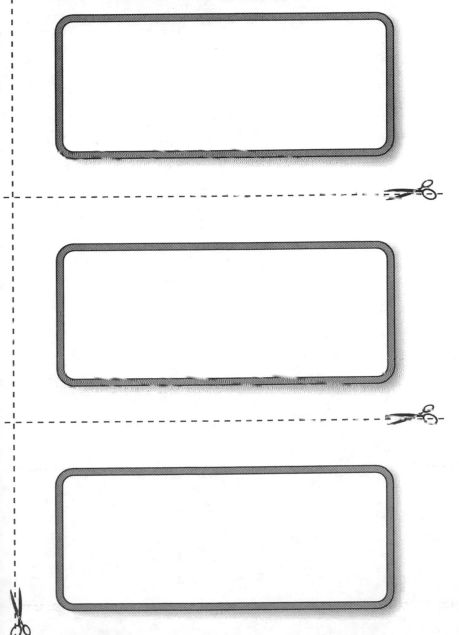

Correct Answers

Blank Cards for *Your Own Questions*

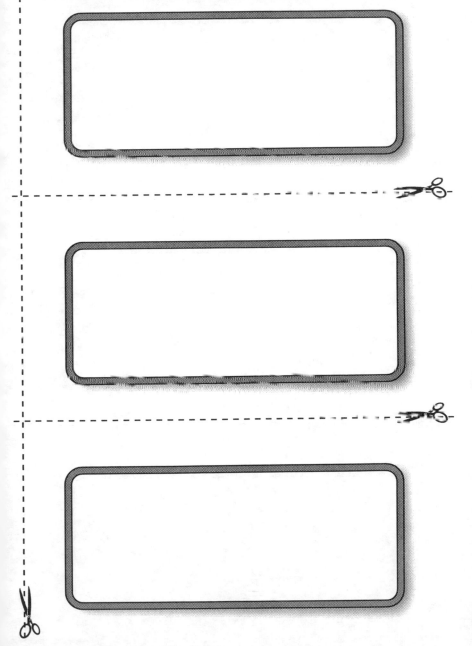

Correct Answers

Blank Cards for *Your Own Questions*

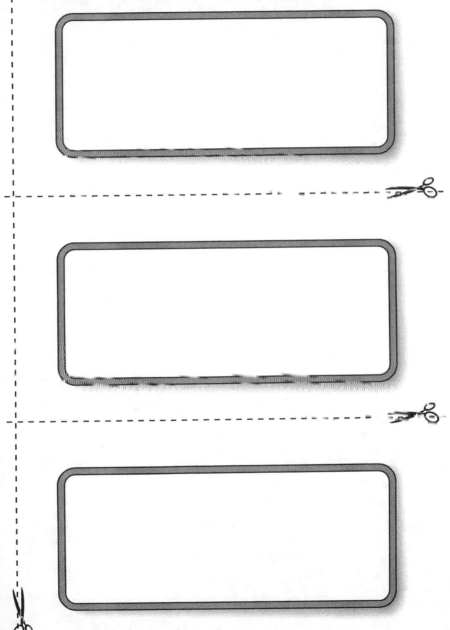

Correct Answers

Blank Cards for
Your Own Questions

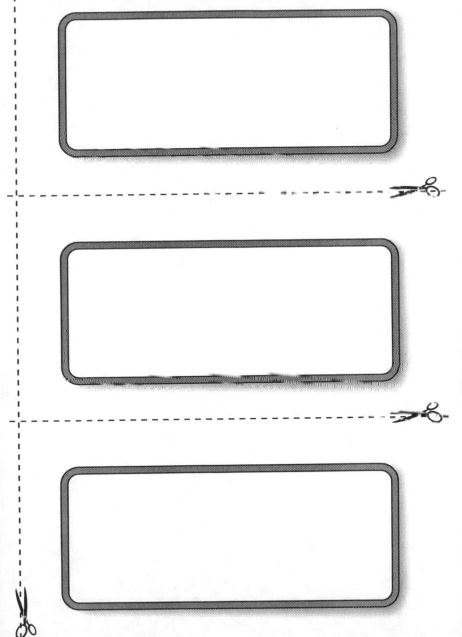

Correct Answers

Blank Cards for
Your Own Questions

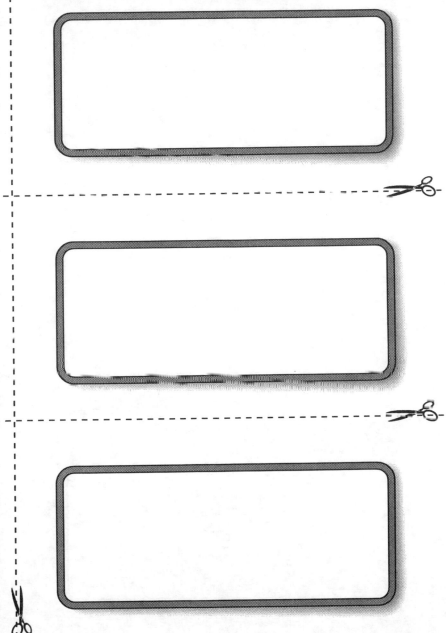

Correct Answers

Blank Cards for
Your Own Questions

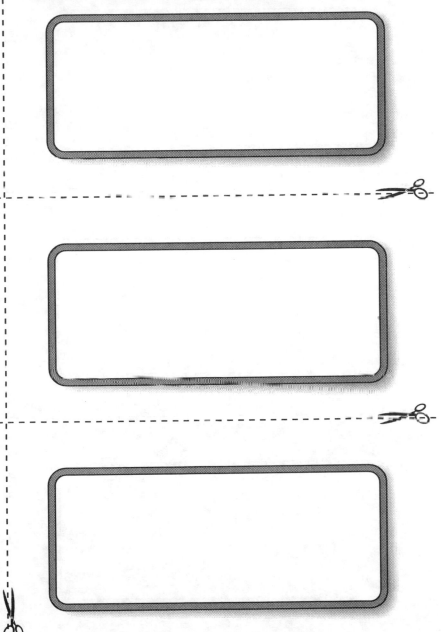

Correct Answers

Blank Cards for
Your Own Questions

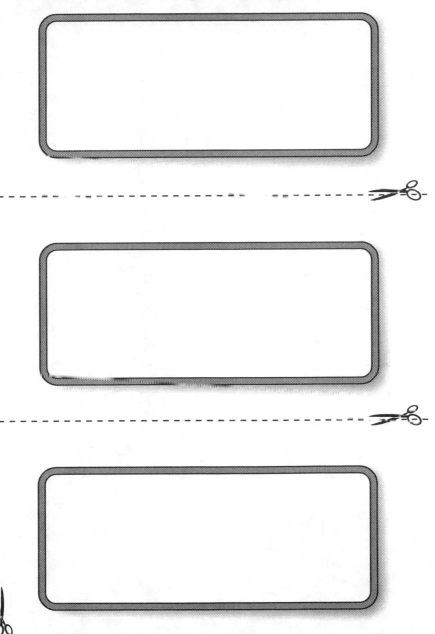

Correct Answers

Blank Cards for
Your Own Questions

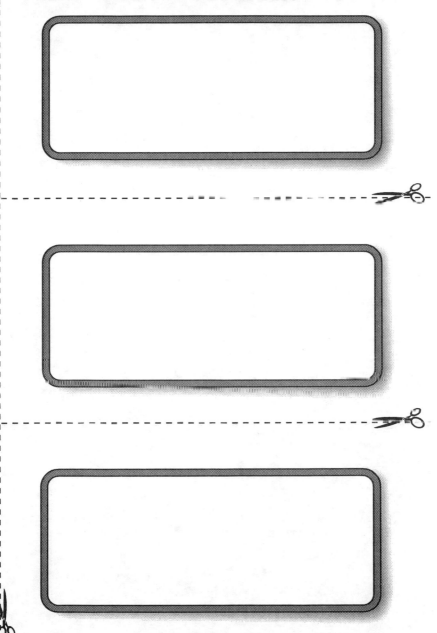

Correct Answers

Blank Cards for
Your Own Questions

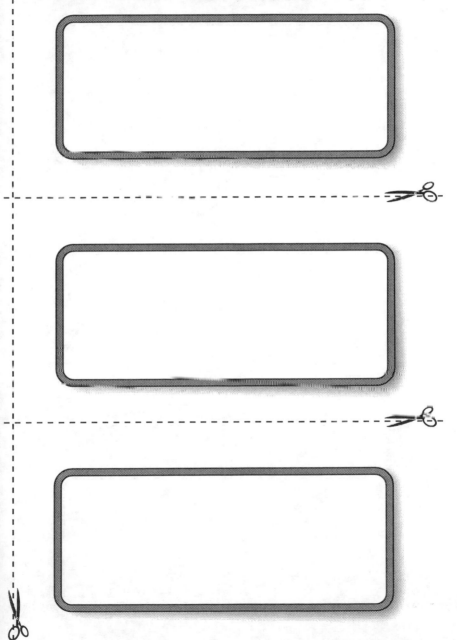

Correct Answers

Blank Cards for
Your Own Questions

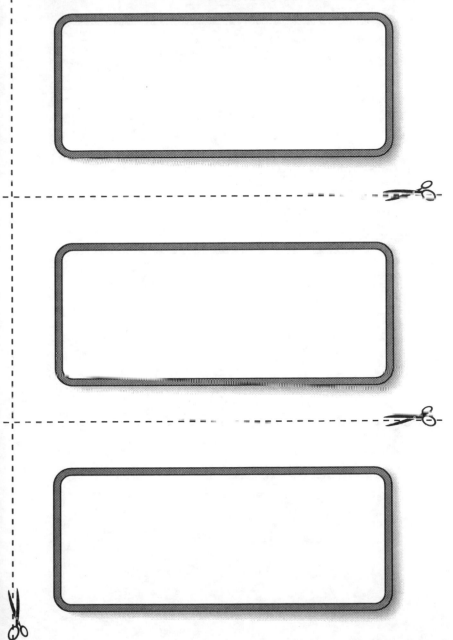

Correct Answers

Blank Cards for
Your Own Questions

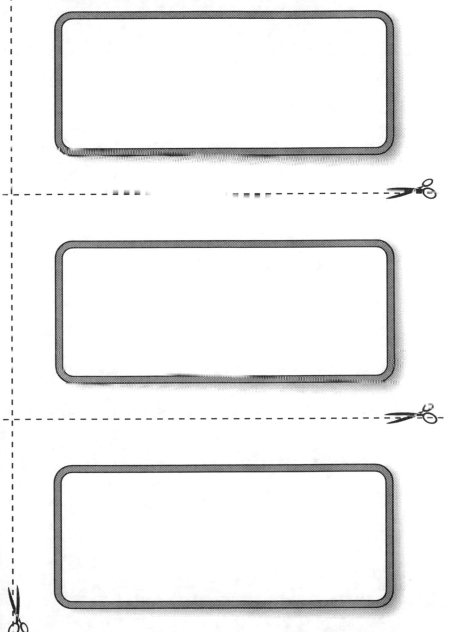

Correct Answers

Blank Cards for
Your Own Questions

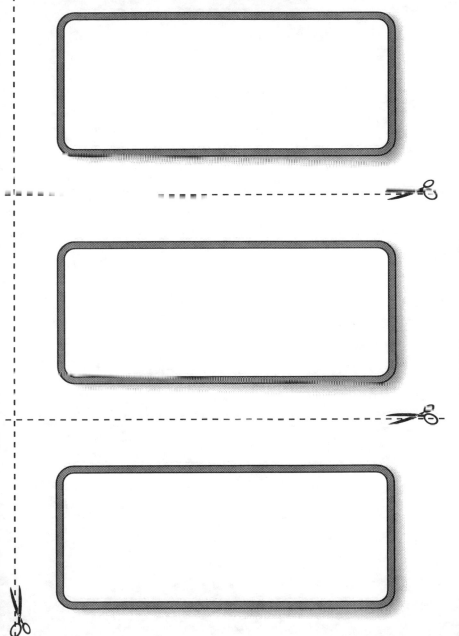

Correct Answers

Blank Cards for *Your Own Questions*

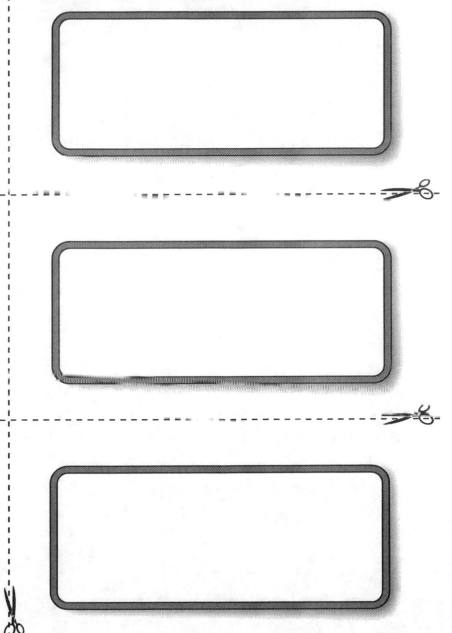

Correct Answers

Blank Cards for *Your Own Questions*

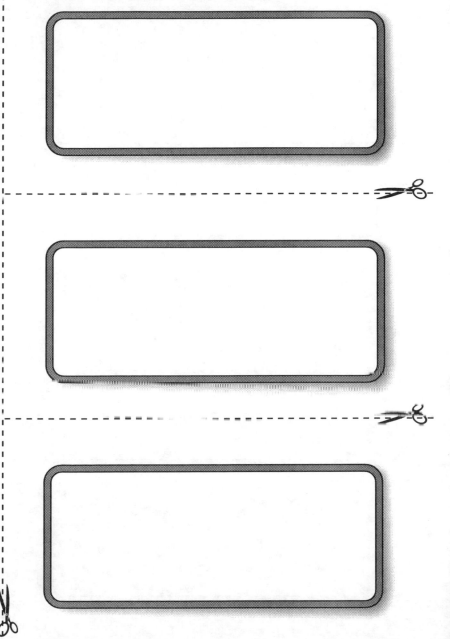

Correct Answers

Blank Cards for
Your Own Questions

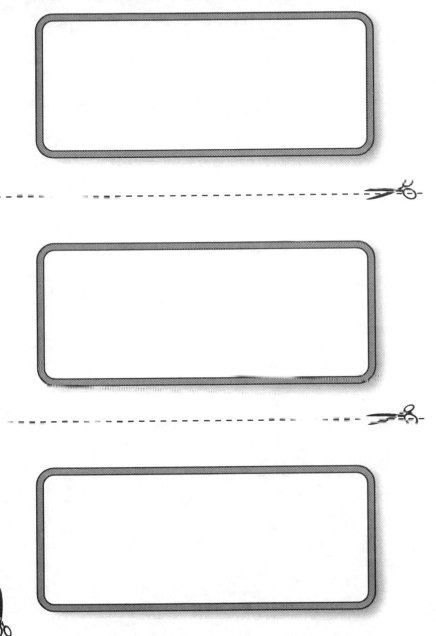

Correct Answers

Blank Cards for
Your Own Questions

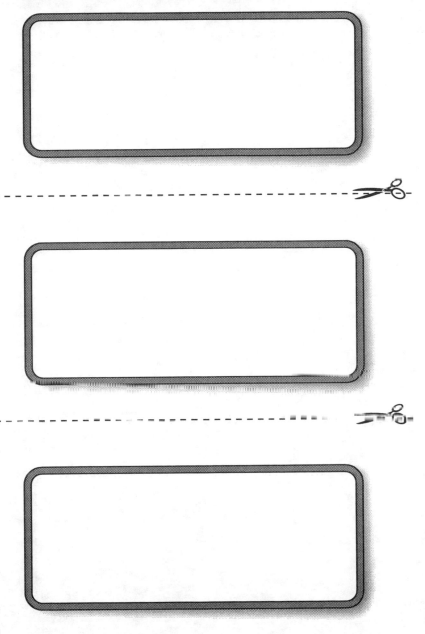

Correct Answers

Blank Cards for
Your Own Questions

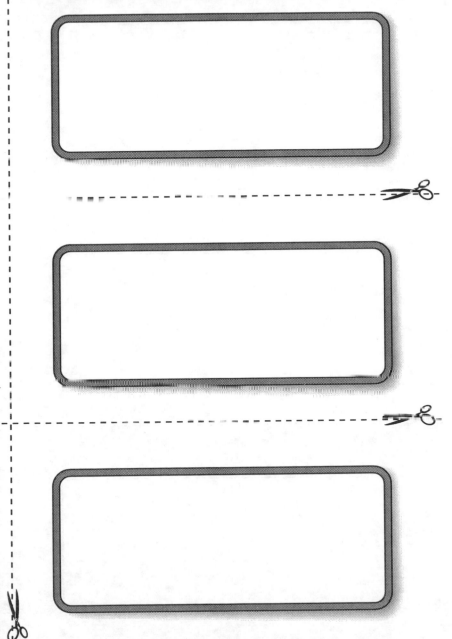

Correct Answers

INDEX

defamation, 666
defensible, 609
deferential, 17
deign, 529
deleterious, 658
deliberate, 57
delineate, 701
demise, 366
deplete, 167
depravity, 305
deprecate, 229
depredation, 230
derogatory, 435
desecrate, 581
despoil, 278
determinate, 324
devoid, 156
dexterous, 68
diffuse, 494
digress, 600
dilettante, 680
din, 519
disapprobation, 405
disarray, 3
disavow, 103
discerning, 114
discourse, 585
discreet, 387
disdain, 147
disentangle, 101
disingenuous, 18
disinterested, 97
disparate, 140
disperse, 214
disputatious, 25
disseminate, 182
dissonance, 568
diverse, 62
docile, 672
doggerel, 412
dogma, 26
dogmatic, 457

dormant, 676
dowdy, 330
dregs, 188
ebullience, 343
eclectic, 24
edifice, 115
edify, 65
effervescence, 168
effigy, 191
effluvium, 602
effrontery, 193
egocentric, 388
egress, 73
ellipsis, 356
eloquence, 185
elusive, 552
eminence, 601
emulate, 49
encroach, 537
encumber, 162
endorse, 27
enigma, 384
ephemeral, 56
epicure, 298
epigram, 172
epiphany, 636
epitome, 444
equanimity, 48
equivocation, 502
errant, 448
erratic, 536
esoteric, 565
estimable, 135
ethereal, 12
eulogy, 209
euphony, 434
evanescent, 592
evasion, 226
evoke, 380
exculpate, 634
execute, 450
exemplary, 180

vicissitude, 611
vigilance, 659
vilify, 303
virile, 108
virulent, 499
visage, 169
viscid, 20
viscous, 641
vitiate, 151
vitriolic, 217
vivacious, 224
volatile, 308
volition, 431
voracious, 639
waive, 34
wan, 332
wanton, 438

warrant, 576
welter, 160
whimsical, 513
wily, 16
wizened, 608
wooden, 280
workaday, 447
wreak, 138
wrest, 509
wretched, 476
wry, 290
xenophobia, 241
yoke, 99
yore, 419
zealot, 508
zenith, 399